LIFE IS A BLESSING

Dale Evans Rogers

Life

IS A

Blessing

**A Heartfelt Collection
of Three Bestselling Works
Complete in One Volume**

ANGEL UNAWARE

SAY YES TO TOMORROW

OUR VALUES

Inspirational Press, New York

Contents

Angel Unaware

DALE EVANS ROGERS

Foreword

BY NORMAN VINCENT PEALE

$\mathcal{M}$y daughter Elizabeth and I had been all-out fans of Roy Rogers and Dale Evans long before we knew them as personal friends. We loved their movie and TV adventures, but that wasn't all; we sensed something fine and wholesome in what they said and did, in their dynamic personalities, in the radiant joy and lovable humility that is so much a part of them.

Then they started coming to New York for their rodeo in Madison Square Garden, and every Sunday morning I saw them in my congregation at Marble Collegiate Church. We returned the compliment by attending the rodeo. We were thrilled as they raced about the arena and as Roy sang "Peace in the Valley"—a song that is half ballad and half hymn. But we were moved deeply when he said to the youngsters in *his* "congregation," "I hear some kid says it is sissy stuff to go to Sunday school. Don't you believe him. Sunday school is for he-men." The awe with which the children accepted this convinced me that cowboys are often more effective preachers than the preachers themselves.

Their business is entertainment; their purpose is to speak for God in their daily work. By their words, their kindliness, their uprightness, and their love of people, they turn the minds of everyone they meet to God—a rare and beautiful accomplishment, in our kind of world!

Dale Evans does just that, in this little book. She is a mother who has won great victory over great sorrow. When she first told me the story you will read here, I realized that I was hearing of an amazing experience and standing in the presence of a great soul. I saw at once that Robin, her baby, had not lived and died in vain. Where most babies die and leave the mother crushed, Robin put on immortality and her mother found the very joy of God in what might otherwise have been an overwhelming tragedy.

The sweetness, the touching humor and spiritual understanding with which little Robin Rogers talks with God in this book will comfort and strengthen all who

read it, as they did me when I read the manuscript—
through misty eyes.

This is one book I'll never forget.

Preface

When I was in high school I dreamed of being a writer, as English, Grammar, and Composition were my favorite subjects. Little did I realize that my writing career would be forged in the crucible of tragedy.

On August 26, 1950, my husband, Roy Rogers, and I became the parents of a baby girl, Robin Elizabeth, who was called "Little Angel" by her Daddy. Had we not been committed Christians when told she was mongoloid and would be retarded, the news would have totally destroyed us, since we are quite vulnerable to the needs of children.

When advised to put our Robin in a foster home, one that understood the plight of the Down's syndrome child, Roy said, "We are taking our baby home. God has a purpose for allowing this, and if we put her away, we will never know it." As for myself, I could not imagine putting away any child of mine.

Romans 8:28 declares, "All things work together for good to them that love God, to them who are the called according to his purpose."

How I thank our God for the two years He let us minister to our little angel, for she really was the "cementer" of our Christian commitment.

In the ensuing years since this little epistle of love was published, Robin has spread her wings in an amazing way. Prior to the advent of her little book, children with Down's syndrome were seldom, if ever, seen in public by curious eyes. Six months after Fleming H. Revell published *Angel Unaware*, these little children, by the score, were brought to theaters where we appeared, to see us. We saw them in the crowds of parade spectators, in stores—in many public places. Churches began Sunday-school classes for these special little ones, who have been called "those nearest to the heart of God." Grants were made for college and university scholarships in special education. Public schools were permitted to have special classrooms for those considered educable. Medical science has taken a fresh look at options for treating these children at birth, to help them get a better start. Then along came the Special Olympics—a beautiful blessing for these children and their parents. Indeed, we appreciate the confidence God placed in us, to send Robin our way. Every time I see a Down's syndrome child at work in school, sheltered workshops, or in routine jobs offered in many organizations, I can almost see Robin's beautiful, beautiful smile....

My heartfelt appreciation to the late, beloved Dr. Frank S. Mead, for his superb editing of material that tumbled onto notebooks, newspaper margins, the backs of radio scripts—from the very full heart of a loving, grieving mother. This book was started just two days after Robin's funeral by the urgent prodding of God....

My thanks to Dr. Norman Vincent Peale, who was kind enough to write the original foreword, and to the Fleming H. Revell Company, which dared to take on a subject no other publisher would touch with a ten-foot pole. Over a million copies have been sold since the spring of 1952, and I pray it will go on and on—as long as the "angels unaware" visit this vale of tears.

Sincerely,
Dale Evans Rogers

Be not forgetful to entertain strangers:
for thereby some have entertained angels unawares.

Hebrews 13:2

Oh Father, it's good to be home again. I thought sometimes that You had forgotten me, Down There. Two years Up Here doesn't seem like much, but on earth it can be a long, long time—and it was long, and often hard, for all of us.

When You lifted me up from the earth, just a few minutes ago, it was Sunday, and my Mommy and Daddy were crying, and everything seemed so dark and sad and confused. And all of a sudden it was bright and clear and happy, and I was in Your arms. Was it the same way for them Down There, Father? You can put me down, now;

I'm perfectly all right, now that I'm rid of that lump of hindering clay....

That music sounds nice—it's even nicer than the music I heard Down There. I guess a lot of people didn't know it, but Down There I had as much music as I had pain. I had my own little red radio, and my nurse let me play it whenever I wanted to. And I had the sweetest little white woolly horse, with tunes in his tummy, and he played for me every night on my pillow, right before I went to sleep. Of course, I loved horses, maybe because Daddy was a cowboy and loved them, too.

Mommy often took me in to play on the big piano, and I had a little toy piano, too, that I used to pound day and night. It helped.

Yes, there was music. I even heard happy songs that they couldn't hear. They just saw my sickness, and they felt sorry for me. But I knew *why* I was sick, and that because I was sick I could do things for them; and as they say Down There, that was "music to my ears."

It was quite an experience, Father. When You sent me on that earthly mission, I never dreamed what it would be like, or how much We could do, in two short years. We did a lot.

*W*ell, on August 26, 1950 (Earth time) I woke up in a place they called a "hospital," and I could see people in white robes standing all around. Just like it is Up Here, Father—white robes all around. One of them, a nurse, said, "She's blue." I didn't know what that meant, but I did know that everything was going according to the Plan. They said something about a cord being wrapped around my neck, and they slipped that off, and I felt more comfortable. They spanked me a little to make me cry (and laughed while they did it!), and then they put me in a funny little thing called an "oxygen box," and the doctor turned away from me to help the woman on the table. That was my earthly mother.

She opened her eyes and turned to look at me, and she said, "Hi, Robin. You're beautiful!" Then they wheeled her out to her own room, to rest.

The doctor came back to me and looked at me, hard. He seemed so worried about me that I started worrying about *him*. Some other doctors and nurses came and stood looking down at me and whispering among themselves, and they started doing all sorts of odd things to me to make me move around.

They told one another that something was wrong, because I didn't "respond" to their "tests" like the other babies did. Poor souls! I could have told them that this, too, was part of the Plan. But they couldn't know that— they didn't have eyes to see You there beside me, or ears to hear Your voice.

They didn't realize that You provide certain conditions in order to accomplish some wonderful purpose. A lot of them Down There don't understand yet, Father, that You always have a blessing in mind, in everything You plan. Many mothers with babies like me wouldn't be so bitter and so heartbroken if they just knew You and Your ways better.

The doctor who "delivered" me came back. (I like that word *delivered*; it makes the doctors seem like Your agents, or Your "mailmen" Down There.) He brought three children's doctors (called "pediatricians")—and how they did talk! And shake their heads! I heard one of the nurses say, "She has mongoloid eyes." I wondered what *mongoloid* meant. They seemed to think it was something awful.

Art Rush was there, too; he's Daddy's manager and closest friend, and he said, "So what? There's nothing unusual about that. Her Daddy has almond-shaped eyes, and he's not ashamed of them, and his father and his grandfather had them. It runs in the family." There was quite an argument about all this, but I didn't take much interest in it. Why should I worry? I knew it had all been arranged....

I had a pretty hard time getting started; they had to give me oxygen for the first few days.

I guess Mommy didn't know about all this fuss, because when they took me in to see her, she was so happy. She patted my face and kissed me over and over and one day she prayed to You, while she held me in her arms, and promised You that she would help me to grow up to be a good Christian. I liked that. I knew We were on the right track.

Daddy came at visiting hours and stood looking at me through the glass, laughing and jumping all around, making funny signs, and looking proud. I heard him say once that I had little ears, like Mommy's. They were happy about me, all right.

*B*ut the doctors and nurses weren't so happy. They were all dreading the time when they'd have to tell Mommy and Daddy about the bad shape I was in. Whenever Mommy got to boasting about me to her nurse, the nurse would change the subject. That happened several times, and Mommy began to get suspicious. Finally she asked the nurse right out if there was anything wrong with me, and the nurse looked away and said she wasn't allowed to discuss my "condition."

One day the nurse slipped; she said that the doctor had said something about my being a "borderline" baby.

Mommy's face went white, and she asked the nurse, "Did he say...*mongoloid?*" I felt so sorry for that nurse! She didn't know what to say then, and she tried to make the best of it by saying, "Don't be worried. There is only a thin line between genius and insanity. Some handicapped children have turned out to be exceptionally brilliant. They can go —either way."

When the doctor came, Mommy went for him! He was a good doctor; he had a big heart under that white coat. He said he just wasn't sure yet, and he hadn't said anything to Mommy because he didn't want to worry her before she got on her feet, but I hadn't responded very well to *some* of their tests. Otherwise I was "all right"— and I had rallied quite well in the last two days. But my "muscle tone" was poor, I had trouble swallowing my food, and I seemed to be listless. He said that symptoms like these, at birth, *sometimes* meant the baby might not develop as it should.

Mommy asked him what she and Daddy should do. What did anybody do with a mongoloid baby? Doctor said gently that there wasn't much anyone could do; the few institutions for such babies were overcrowded, and the state homes and hospitals wouldn't take in "one of these children" until he was four years old. Then he said something fine:

"Take her home and love her. Love will help more than anything else in a situation like this—more than all the hospitals and all the medical science in the world." That's one thing I learned Down There, Father—that the doctors are just beginning to discover how much help You are in *any* situation. They're beginning to talk seriously about "tender, loving care." You are getting through to the doctors.

When the doctor left, Mommy started to cry. She said there should be *some* place for babies like me. Why didn't somebody do something about it? Maybe—and my heart missed a beat when I heard her say it—maybe it was high time the Rogers did something about starting a foundation for handicapped babies. I loved that—not because it could help me, but because it looked like the first fruit of my mission Down There. Because I had come to them, they were already planning to help others like me!

But Mommy kept on crying, and Daddy said, "Don't cry. God will take care of her; she's in His hands, and His hands are big enough to hold her. We will pray and trust Him."

That was just like my Daddy. He has always trusted You, but You know, he did get to wondering sometimes. He didn't doubt that everything was being taken care of from Up Here—not that. Daddy had been a Christian for some time before I came, but like most people Down There, he saw things that hurt his heart, and he couldn't help asking questions.

It always hurt him to see little crippled children, and

he'd ask, "Why? *Why?* Where's God? I know He's a loving God, but if He loves these children, why does He let them suffer?" A lot of folks ask these questions, Father, and a lot of them never seem to get any answers. Daddy did!

He began to read his Bible as though he had never seen it before. And he prayed, more and more often. I could see the change in his face; it was quiet now. He seemed to be getting hold of himself. We were getting to him, Father; a new Roy Rogers was being born.

They took me "home," to the house in the Hollywood Hills.

$\mathcal{T}$here was a sweet nurse named Donna waiting for me when we got home——and the brother and sisters You sent on ahead of me. My brother Dusty ran up to the nurse who was holding me and said, "Can I see the baby?" He put his finger on my forehead and asked, "Is she real?" And Cheryl and Linda laughed and cooed over me and said the nicest things to me, and they thought I was wonderful. They didn't see anything wrong. Children never do. They have clear, sharp eyes that look 'way down, and what they see is always beautiful.

Donna was like that, too; she had brought Dusty through the first six months of his life, and she kept telling Mommy and Daddy that I was going to be all right. She was speaking the truth and didn't realize it! Once she asked Mommy if "Rh negative blood factor" had anything to do with the way I turned blue when I tried to take milk out of the bottle. Mommy said the doctors had told her that the Rh factor had nothing to do with my condition.

Poor Donna slipped and fell and broke her wrist, so another sweet, motherly nurse named Jo came to take care of me.

They put me in a contraption called a "bassinet" and tried hard to make me drink that milk. I had a hard time of it; I couldn't seem to get enough suction. It made me so tired, and my whole left arm would turn blue. And my head was wobbly as anything! I just couldn't seem to control it. Mommy worried over that; they almost had to tie her in bed to keep her from coming in and standing over me, looking anxious.

The milk business was bad enough, but when I was three weeks old, a doctor examined me and found I had developed a heart murmur. He said he was afraid of that; it was just another "mongoloid symptom." He said he always advised parents, in situations like this, to put the baby in a "home"; they'd have to give the child up sometime, anyway, and it was easier to do it quickly, before the child became entrenched in their hearts. He said that mothers gave children like this all their attention and were likely to neglect the other children in the family. He was a kind man, and he meant well, but what he said left Mommy so stunned she couldn't answer.

Daddy said, "No! We'll keep her and do all we can for her and take our chances." Mommy smiled then; she was glad, and she said what I had been waiting for her to say: that You had sent me for some special reason, and they had no right to cast aside anything or anyone You had sent.

She said she was sorry for other parents who had babies like me. Father, it *is* hard. It was hard for Daddy and Mommy—but worth every tear and heartache it cost! I saw what was happening: already, they were beginning to appreciate Your Cross....

*M*ommy kept trying to make me smile. The pediatrician kept asking her, "Has she smiled yet?" He said if a baby didn't smile until he was three months old, it meant that he was at least 50 percent retarded in his mental growth. Mommy didn't want to leave me, for anything, until she saw that smile.

Oh, Father, she and Jo tried so hard to make me smile! Mommy worked overtime on that. I was never out of her thoughts. She was too "possessive" about me, and that wasn't good.

Of course, there was a reason for that. Mommy had always been "career minded." Even when she was a young girl she wanted to succeed, and succeed *big*, in show business, and for a long time she put that career before everything else in her life. But after I arrived, it didn't seem to mean so much to her, after all.

We took care of that "success" business in short order, didn't We? She seemed to be trying to push all thought of her career out of her mind, so as to have more room in her mind for me. She was always praying for me, always hovering over me. Then she realized that giving me all her time and attention might be bad, too; there were other children in the house, and it wasn't fair to them. She tried to share her time and her love with Dusty and Cheryl and Linda and Daddy and to go on with her work.

It was quite a struggle she went through, trying to find out what You wanted her to do about all this. You used a mighty hot fire in purging her for Our use, Father, but the flame was healing, too.

Daddy was trying to learn, too.

Just before they left to go on tour, Daddy came into my room with a funny-looking thing called a "camera." He ran the window shades up high; Your sun hit my weak eyes full force, and I set up quite a howl. Daddy went ahead and took a lot of pictures of me; he loved pictures and cameras. He wasn't satisfied to take pictures inside; he had to take me out on the porch and "shoot" some more.

He was a lot of fun, my Daddy—everyone loved him Down There. He was so young in spirit—just like a boy—and after I came he seemed younger than ever. You wouldn't believe it, but he was often shy and nervous when he faced crowds. But not after he got to reading his Bible and studying me! After a while he was relaxed, confident, sure of himself, and not nervous at all. I think it was because he came to understand that Your arms were always beneath him, as they were beneath me, and that You wouldn't let either one of us fall.

I loved him the first time I saw him, and many a time I wished I could have a heart-to-heart talk with him, because he was trying so hard to find out what You had in mind. I think he'd been trying to find out about that before. We went to work on him, because once I heard him say that his big success came to him because of all the letters he got from boys and girls, saying they prayed for him. Now his idea of success was changing; We were teaching him that real success was *spiritual*.

He was changing, all right. The old question about why God let innocent children suffer didn't seem to bother him very much anymore. Bless his heart, he was learning that it isn't really we innocent children who suffer, it's the ones around us who suffer while they're learning to be obedient to Your will.

Mommy was always trying to figure it out—to find some reason for my "affliction." Sometimes she said maybe it was part of the Plan to send Daddy and her an afflicted child so Daddy could understand all afflicted children; other times she thought it was because of some old sin or sins—and then she would think of some wonderful Christian having the same trouble she was having and she'd ask, "Why?" and get all mixed up again.

But getting mixed up a little doesn't matter, does it, Father? Anybody who thinks gets confused, sooner or later. But I noticed Down There that those who tried to think out things about You and Your ways usually found a way out of their confusion. It was those who didn't care enough to think at all that I felt sorry for. I always thought it was the not caring and not thinking that was sinful, not the being confused.

*W*hen I was two months old, my parents had to go off on one of those "personal appearance" tours, and they took me out to Jo's house, where it was nice and dry and sunny. It was cold and damp in the Hollywood Hills, and Mommy didn't think that would be good for me. She and Daddy were finishing up a "recording" of a radio broadcast, but they came out to see me the very next day.

That day there was a consultation with two doctors. They said I had a very bad heart condition, and that I probably wouldn't live very long, but for Mommy and Daddy to go ahead with the tour, because nothing would happen for six months, anyway. Mommy asked why they couldn't operate on my heart, and they said no operation could help.

When she heard that, Mommy cried; Daddy told her again, "It's up to God now. Let's leave it with Him." Mommy said she knew that—but she would fight to the last ditch to help me until You called for me. Of course, she was still fighting herself....

I'm glad they had to go on that tour—glad they had to go out and entertain people, because while they were so busy making those other people happy, they wouldn't worry about me. Up Here we know that if we want to be happy we have to make others happy; Down There, they haven't quite caught up with that idea. But they will.

I guess Mommy would have collapsed if it hadn't been for the rule that "the show must go on."

They called every night while they were away; Mommy was overjoyed the night Jo told her I had "laughed right out loud" that day. Everybody in the house laughed with me, they were so glad—my aunts and grandparents and brother and sisters and Ginny, Dusty's nurse, and our nice housekeeper Emily. They were good to me—so good that sometimes I got to wishing my mission could go on a little longer. But every time that happened—every time I got "earth minded"—I would start thinking of You and of how nice it was Up Here. That was when they said I had "a faraway look" in my eyes, and they'd try to snap me out of it. It *was* a faraway look; I was seeing things they couldn't see, and I pitied them. Someday they'll know; someday they'll see clearly, instead of in their misty mirrors.

They loved me, all of them, and maybe when I laughed it was in joy and thankfulness for their love. They weren't ashamed of their little "borderline" mongoloid! A lot of parents are, You know. They whisk them off somewhere to keep them hidden, so others won't know. That's partly because they want to shelter these children from the eyes of curious people, and partly because of their own pride.

Pride! I got so sick of that, Down There. It's an ugly weed, Father, growing all over the place. And there's nothing like having a handicapped child to strip the pride and pretense from a pair of parents. I guess it's all right for a father to throw out his chest and boast about how smart his boy Jim is, but it's wrong when he tries to send thanks Up Here because his children are just a little better than any other children. It's really good when You send a handicapped baby to people like that; it takes them down a peg or two, and their real character begins to show, and they begin to be the kind of people You want them to be.

Mommy and Daddy went to one of the finest medical clinics in the world during this tour, and they showed the top man my picture and told him what the other doctors had said. He took one look and asked, "Is she a good baby?"

"Oh, yes!" said Mommy.

"And is she always in a relaxed position, like this picture shows?"

"Most of the time, yes."

"Then you have a real problem," he said. "There's absolutely nothing we can do—for the heart or for anything else. *There is no help.*"

He told Mommy that this affliction was no respecter of persons, that it hits anywhere, anytime. One of his friends, a top baby doctor, had a baby just like me. He advised Mommy to put me in a home, before her heart broke.

Mommy wouldn't listen to it. I'm glad she didn't, because if she had, she and Daddy might have missed Your point completely.

$\mathcal{T}$he day before they got home, Jo got a "virus," and had to leave me. Daddy and Mommy came "on the double," scared half out of their wits that I'd get the virus, too, and they started hunting for a new nurse. They had to record another radio broadcast that week, so You can imagine the confusion around the house. Mommy called doctors, hospitals, nurses' agencies—everything, and no nurse could be found, for love or money. They were really scared, for I was hard to feed, and my head seemed more wobbly than ever. But they found a nurse. Funny, isn't it, how things always work out, Down There? People fall all over themselves while You're working it out....

Art Rush (that's Daddy's manager, remember?) called up and said he knew a lady who could help me. They sent for here, and she came and talked to Mommy and told her I could be healed, no matter what the doctors said—that God could do that. She said she knew a nurse who would take me, but Mommy would have to consent to having me live at the nurse's house for a few months—where she wouldn't have to contend with Mommy's fearful thoughts about me. She said that babies felt fear, that Mommy was putting her fear into me, and that would hold me back.

You can imagine what Mommy said. NO! A big, loud, furious NO! She sat down and began telephoning all over, looking for another nurse. Of course she didn't find one. She wasn't supposed to, according to the Plan....

Finally she said, "Oh, all right. But this nurse will have to spend a few days at our house first, so we can see how she and Robin get along."

So the new nurse came; I called her "Cau-Cau," and she took charge of me just like she'd known me all my life. Mommy relaxed and let me go.

Cau-Cau knew her business with babies. She told Mommy I wasn't really her child; I was God's child. She said I was with You before I came to her, that Mommy should be glad to give me back to You, and that You'd take care of me.

The lady who got this nurse for Mommy said the same thing, and she said that Mommy should never think of me as an imperfect child but as a child perfect in Your eyes.

They were part of the Plan, all right. They were doing just what You sent them to do.

I shared a nice sunny room with Cau-Cau in her home, and I began to feel better. I was stronger, and while I couldn't sit up, my head was steadier, and I was beginning to take some interest in things around me. But I was still pretty nervous; whenever anyone raised his voice, I started to cry. Any noise bothered me.

Father, it's so *noisy* Down There. So much babble and silly racket. What are they trying to do, anyway? Are they noisy because they're afraid of something, or what?

They worried about my "coordination," which certainly wasn't too good. From the time I began to notice bright objects, they would try to make me pick up rattles and toys. You should have heard Mommy the day she was writing down a telephone number, and I grabbed the pencil out of her hand and started scribbling all over the notebook. Right away, she got me crayons and a big drawing book to encourage me. She bubbled over every time I showed the least sign of improvement. She was still hoping....

Cau-Cau used to say that I had "such loving hands... always stretched out to give... not earthly, grasping hands, and that's heavenly!" Of course, my hands were loving. They were filled with Your love, so they could bless those around me.

She and Mommy were worried about my little narrow foot. Cau-Cau said they would have to have my shoes "specially made." I had to choke down a giggle, because Up Here we don't need "specially made shoes" at all. Matter of fact, we don't need anything, Here. What a blessing that is!

Humans worry too much. If they could somehow trust more and worry less, they'd have heaven on earth, wouldn't they? I wanted to talk to them about that, and sometimes I got so anxious about it that I would start to jabber a mile a minute. They would stare at me and try to understand what I was trying to say, and—forgive me, Father, but I'm afraid I lost my patience with them. You know, I loved them, and I wanted to have them understand, and I hated to see them groping.

Mommy used to hold me on her lap to listen to a religious program on the radio; I heard her whisper that she hoped I'd "somehow understand." Poor heart—if she only knew how much I understood!

It seemed like *everybody* came out to see me on my first Christmas. Mommy brought me a doll in a bright red dress, and I loved it. My grandfather and grandmother and my uncle came, too, and there were my great big grown-up brother Tom and his wife, Barbara. He had the kindest eyes; I looked in those eyes and saw You.

They all played with me until I got pretty tired and started to perspire, and nurse said they'd better go. They all had tears in their eyes when they left, and I wanted to cheer them up. I wanted to say, "This is Christmas, and you should be glad. The angels sang for the Babe in the manger, and they're singing for me. Can't you hear it? *Listen!*" But my balky old tongue wouldn't behave....

Mommy came to see me almost every day, and I don't thing Cau-Cau approved of that, but she couldn't do anything about it. Mommy said she intended to see me whenever she had the chance. And she said our family was moving out to a ranch at Encino, in the valley, and she was going to build a little house for me and Cau-Cau, because she wanted me at home.

Cau-Cau said she'd come, "for a little while, until Robin gets used to living with all those people," and Daddy and Grampy and my great uncle started building it right away....

I was ten months old when we moved into that house. It was pretty, with two rooms and a bath; my room was blue, like my eyes, and there were frilly white curtains at the windows. It made you happy just to look at it.

The new ranch was really something. Daddy had lots of dogs, and Cau-Cau would wheel me out in my go-cart to see them. And there were chickens and ducks and horses and even little foxes and raccoons. I got to know one dog real well; her name was Lana, and when I was fretty or nervous she'd come up and nuzzle me with her cold nose, and I'd feel better. Her fur was a soft gray color, like a dove's, and she had long silky ears that I couldn't help pulling whenever I got my hands on them. Lana didn't mind. Everywhere I went she followed me.

Funny, about that. Children and animals Down There get along fine. They sort of talk to each other....

We had some geese, and were they a noisy bunch! They made a queer hissing sound whenever we came near them, and I learned to make it too; Cau-Cau thought that was smart of me, and she told me so. Some days Cau-Cau would give me a piece of stale bread to feed the chickens, or we'd take a walk over to the next ranch where there was a gentle old horse I loved, and I'd pat his nose, and he'd whinny back to me in horse language.

Cau-Cau read animal books to me at mealtime. That way, I got through the meals. They were hard to take, Father. I never cared much for solid food, and they played all sorts of tricks on me to get me to eat it. Finally they got me a suction-bottom plate and a specially curved spoon, hoping I might find my mouth with it. Every now and then, I did! It was an awful bore, and I got it over with as quickly as possible. It was easier in the mornings, when I was hungry; I was so cranky then that Cau-Cau called me "an impatient little witch." She was right. I was.

When I was bored, I'd cry. Mommy couldn't stand that; she was afraid it would affect my weak heart. But Daddy said it was normal, or "O.K.," for a baby to cry.

My head was a little more "normal" now; I could control it a little better, and I was doing better with my tongue, too. And my legs! I could do things with my legs. From the time I was six months old, I could lift them up straight over my head and throw them out sideways— "doing the splits," Daddy called it. The doctor was afraid I'd throw my hips out of joint doing the splits, so he put a brace between my feet. I know this was supposed to keep me from hurting myself, but how I hated that brace! It made me more nervous than ever. I had to wear that brace constantly during the last four months I was Down There, and it wasn't fun.

They kept praying for me. You know, Father, *thousands* of people, scattered all over the country, prayed for me. One way or another, they heard about me, and they talked to You about me. Once, the whole big Southern Baptist Convention in San Francisco prayed. Didn't You like that?

They had "roundtable" prayers in the home, and it pleased me so that I just couldn't keep quiet. I tried to say the words with them, but the words got all mixed up. But they never scolded me. Seems as though they knew all along I was an angel....

After dinner, Mommy would take me to the big piano and let me play. I tried hard to say "play piano," but it wouldn't come, and the best I could say was "pah-pah." Mommy would play and sing for me, and I used to take her hand and make her play some more; then Cau-Cau would say, "Bedtime!" and I'd throw them all a kiss, and nurse and Mommy tucked me in. I always hated to leave that piano.

Maybe I'm talking too much about myself and not enough about what was happening to Mommy and Daddy. I could see that they were "growing in grace." I heard Mommy say one day that she was coming to believe that the only important thing in this world was a person's relationship to God and his faith in Jesus Christ. Then she said she was actually grateful to You for sending me in my handicapped condition, because I had made her walk close to You. She was always reading her Bible, and when she went off with Daddy to San Francisco to testify to Your love in that big convention, I was proud of them. They were not just talking; they were practicing.

And Daddy! He was more and more interested in *sick* children, and he tried to get to see every sick boy or girl who called for him. They loved him. He wore a big white cowboy hat with a silver band on it—I used to put it on and play peekaboo with him. He got to calling me "Little Angel"—and I knew then that he knew.

$\mathcal{M}$ommy and Daddy worked hard. They left us for two whole weeks to go "on location" for a series of television pictures; Daddy had an accident while he was riding horseback, and we even heard that he'd been killed. Of course he wasn't, but it upset everybody for a little. Down There, Father, bad news travels twice as fast as good news. Why is that? Shouldn't it be the other way 'round?

They were busy making motion pictures from sunrise to sunset—so busy that I wondered whether it was worth their while. Why work so hard just to make a little money and then die?

Then one day I overheard Mommy say something about their work that I hadn't heard them ever say before: she said that if they could get Your message to people, especially to young people, through their movies and television and rodeos—if they could just get in a good word for You this way, it was worth all the hard work. And I watched that idea grow and grow and *grow* in their hearts, all during Our mission.

My first earth birthday came along, and we had a great party. Everybody gave me the nicest presents. I had a cake, and Mommy had a photographer come out and take my picture. The present I liked best was a picture of Jesus holding a little blonde girl in His arms, and mothers holding their babies up for You to bless. It made me so homesick! Mommy hung it at the head of my bed so I could see it before going to sleep and the first thing in the morning when I woke up. She tried to teach me to say "Jesus," but all I could get out was "tay-tay."

Cau-Cau gave me a wonderful present, and she never knew it. She told Mommy that of all the babies she had nursed, she loved me most because I needed her most, and she said I was teaching her to be patient. I laughed and kicked my feet when she said that; I saw the lessons soaking in, all around.

I was standing up most of the time, right then, in nurse's lap, and everybody was so happy about it. But all of a sudden I was awfully sick, and it looked for a while as though my mission was over. I had a "convulsion"; it took me a long time to get over that and when I did, my legs wouldn't hold me up. I couldn't stand up anymore.

Mommy and Daddy were sad about that—but they kept right on, as though nothing had happened. At Christmas we had the happiest party (this was my *second* Christmas); that was when I got my little red piano. Mommy and Daddy went to a midnight service to thank

You for sending me.

Sometimes, it seemed that every day was Christmas, at least to me. They would sit me up in the middle of a big play table and let me roll a lot of brightly colored balls around; I could throw them, Daddy said, "like a big league pitcher." Even when they took me to the "orthopedic" place, to have my "physical therapy," I had fun; I would take a round disk and fit it over a rounded piece of wood, and Mommy would play "catch" with the disks and do all sorts of things to keep me interested, so I would try to stand up. I got so I could stand for five whole minutes.

Cheryl, my oldest sister, played the piano. She had studied only a few months, but she could play almost anything at first sight. I loved to sit on her lap while she played fast, happy music. It would excite me so much that I'd grab her hands to make her play faster....

They all laughed at me when I watched the ice skaters on television; I'd sway with them, and when the skaters came up close on the screen, I'd wave to them. It was all done silently—but what voices there were in that silence, for me!

Emily, our housekeeper, laughed over the wristwatch business. I had a weakness for wristwatches, and when Emily would say, "What time is it, Robin?" I'd hold up my wrist to her, just like I was wearing one. Emily played peekaboo with me over her coffee cup. She seemed to see something deep in me....

*W*ell, spring came, nice and warm, and with spring came Nancy. You know Nancy—she's Your other little angel who lives near us. She's ten now and going strong on *her* mission. She's had thirty-five operations on her legs, but oh, Father, how happy she is, and how happy she's made the people around her! When I saw her, I saw You again, and I felt all warm and good inside. Nancy has lifted her own mother up for a fresh new look into heaven —and she has helped lift my own Mommy, too.

I was so glad to learn that You had introduced Nancy to Mommy before I got there; she'd been a "fan" of ·

Mommy's and Daddy's for some time, and a good friend of my sisters, Linda and Cheryl. Nancy's mother looked at me and she said, "Robin is straight from heaven. I see it in her eyes—just as I see it in Nancy's."

She told Mommy that I had a great work to do Down There and that she and Daddy were lucky to have a part in that work. She also told Mommy about a doctor "up north" who had helped little children like me, and Mommy said she'd take Cau-Cau and me to see him just as soon as they got back from a rodeo engagement in Houston, Texas.

Just as soon as they got back. They knew I'd be there when they got back.

They had me "christened" before they left for Houston, because to Mommy, right at this particular time, it seemed more important than anything else in the world to have me dedicated to You. So they made arrangements with the minister, dressed me up in a white organdy dress (fit for an angel!) with a pink sash, and some new white shoes, and Cau-Cau curled my hair and put a ribbon on my "topknot" (a sort of halo, You know), and away we went.

Art Rush was there; he said he wouldn't miss *this* for anything. And nurse went along, too. I think I got the greatest thrill of all when the minister reached out and took me in his arms. Mommy gave me to him so gladly; she seemed to be saying in her heart, "Here she is, God. I give her to You. I won't fight anymore; I won't try to keep her so much to myself. She's Yours. Take her."

The minister took me in his arms and held me, and I looked up into that kind, patient, loving face and saw You again. Mommy and Daddy were so happy about it that I knew *they* knew You were standing there with them.

Then Mommy and Daddy went off to the Houston rodeo—and what a show that turned out to be! You know, Daddy comes tearing out into the arena on Trigger, and the kids all shout and howl and cheer, and then Daddy talks to them. He tells them never to get the idea in their little heads that there's anything sissy about going to Sunday school and church. He'll say, "Now let's give a big hand to everybody who's going to church on Sunday!" In a *rodeo*, Father! Rodeos are supposed to be tough and wild and woolly. Daddy makes them something a lot finer than that.

Even in that big Madison Square Garden, in New York City, he gets down off Trigger and sings a song about peace, and it's so quiet You can hear a pin drop, even though You're way off Up Here in heaven. They really listen when Daddy sings about "Peace in the Valley":

Oh, I'm tired and I'm weary, but I must travel on
Till the Lord comes and calls me, calls me away,
Where the morning is bright, and the Lamb is the light,
And the night is as fair as the day.

> *There will be peace in the Valley for me. . .peace in the Valley for me.*

I wonder if Daddy is thinking of *his* peace or mine when he sings that?

> *There's no sadness, no sorrow, no trouble I see!*
> *There'll be peace in the Valley for me!*

No sadness, no sorrow! No crippled children, Father!

> *There the bear will be gentle and the wolf will be tame*
> *And the lion will lie down with the lamb;*
> *There the host from the wild will be led by a child. . .*

A child like *me*, Father?

> *And I'll be changed from this creature that I am.*

Mommy said Daddy had never sung that song so beautifully as he sang it in Houston, and Daddy said that was because it was Your song, not his, and that You were helping him sing it. He had peace—perfect peace. He and Mommy went to a big church in Houston on Sunday and told the folks about it.

They were coming along, Father.

*W*e got ready to go to see the doctor up north—in San Francisco. Just before we left, Mommy took me to a "heart specialist" to see what he would say about that tricky heart of mine. It wasn't that she was looking for miracles to happen, Father; it was just that she thought she should do *everything* to help me, and she thought that it might be Your will to reach down to me through some doctor's hand and make it easier for me.

But—no. That wasn't the way it was to be. The doctor said my heart was already enlarged, seriously, and that they couldn't possibly operate. By the end of the summer, he said, that condition would be "important," and they were to bring me to him again.

Mommy asked this doctor about the doctor in San Francisco, and he said, "I hate to see you go on chasing rainbows like this, but I know you will, so go ahead." We went ahead.

We had a room high up in a hotel, and they had one of those "air raid warnings" while we were there, and I'll never forget it. I thought those whistles would burst my eardrums. How they do make noise, and how people do scamper around like a lot of frightened ants! I just couldn't understand it. Maybe you can explain it to me later, Father. *Why* do they act like that, Down There? It's so foolish to go out of your way to get scared and to create confusion. I listened to the whistles and the shouting, and I thought of Daddy singing Your song about peace, and I asked myself, "What's wrong Down Here, anyway? Why don't they just get Your peace?" Nobody seemed to know. They just went on....

The doctor was a kind man, and he was very honest with Mommy. He said he might help my "muscle tone" with a powder taken from "the pituitary gland of a young calf." (Those doctors use such *big* words!) I was to take one capsule a day, plus a tonic of "B-12," to increase my appetite. He said that would help.

But my heart, he was sure, couldn't be helped. He said he believed that when I was born, a few of the heart cells didn't close properly and left a hole. Three or four months of the pituitary gland extract might help me to get up on my feet and walk, but my heart—no.

Mommy took me out in the city square to see the pigeons. Ah, that was good! I loved to see them leap up into the air so fast, and spread their wings, and glide all around, so high up, wild and free and beautiful, against the deep blue of the sky and the big white fleecy clouds. I reached out my hands to touch them up there, and I thought, "How wonderful it will be when I get my wings back...."

Sorry, Father. I guess I was getting a little impatient.

After we got home, Mommy decided it was time for Cau-Cau to take a little vacation; she needed it, for she'd been with me since I was four months old. Mommy had three weeks' rest now from her television work, so she could take care of me all by herself. She figured she and I would have a wonderful time together in those three weeks...and we did!

It was hard for her, because my brother and sisters needed her, too, but she made out all right. She sang to me a lot during those three weeks, and she told me often that I belonged to You. And she prayed. I'd never heard her pray like that before. One day she said to You:

"God, is it Your purpose to heal my baby? If it is, I'll use that healing to Your glory, and all the rest of my life I'll tell people about it, everywhere I go.

"But if that isn't Your will and what You want, then give me strength to meet it, Lord. Strength to face the future and to finish what Robin has started in all our hearts in this house, strength to get her message across to the world. Just strength, Lord, for whatever You have decided."

Sometimes, she would beg You please to let her stay on earth until You had called me Home, so she could watch over me. That thought seemed to haunt her; it was in her heart, like a sharp knife. The idea of my being alone, without her, made her almost terrified.

Many times, Mommy was asked to write articles for the "magazines," on her faith in You, regarding me. She always said, "I will when the time comes." Unconsciously, she was waiting for Your will to be done. She was waiting to see whether I'd be healed Down There or Up Here— whether I was to find my joy on earth or in heaven. It was right that she should wait, for now that I've left earth, she has a great chance to tell a great story about—Us.

Before long, it was Easter. That's a great time, Down There. They "dress up" especially for the Easter service at church, and people go to church then even if they don't go any other time, and I guess that's good, isn't it? They go all week long before Easter Sunday, too, to celebrate

the Crucifixion and the Resurrection, and there is something real holy about Holy Week. It seems so sad on Good
Friday, and then suddenly it's so bright and glorious on
Easter, when Your Son rose from the dead. Some of the
people are pretty heedless about it, but the meaning of
eternal life gets hold of them, and they're quieter and
better. I think that idea—that I'd go on living in a better
condition than I was in then, and that everything would
work out all right—I think that idea was strong in Mommy
and Daddy and in the whole family that last Easter I had
Down There.

Mommy wheeled me out in my go-cart to watch
Cheryl and Linda and Dusty hunt for Easter eggs. The
"bunny" was supposed to have left them—and Daddy
looked at me and said I looked just like the bunny,
because my knitted cap was white with big ears on the
sides. He got that camera out again!

It was warm now, and Mommy would take me into
the shallow part of our swimming pool. That water was
wonderful. Mommy would hold my arms around her
neck, and I'd kick out, like a little frog, spattering water
all over Cau-Cau. She didn't mind. She loved me. I heard
her say many times, "God is good to have made her so
beautiful."

Beautiful? I guess I was, although when I was born
nobody would have thought it, except maybe my parents.
Isn't it funny, Father, that the first thing people worried

about was my slanted eyes——and by the time I was a year old they were saying, "Hasn't she beautiful eyes?" It's like You say, "All things shall be changed." Even ugly things have a way of changing into beautiful things, under Your hand.

Nurse told us that a friend had said to her, "Never admit that her condition was diagnosed as mongoloid, because even if she turns out all right, people will never give her a chance." But——I was *changed*, and nobody was thinking of me as "mongoloid" but just as a beautiful child. They would look at me and say, "She's a doll," or "She's like a little bird...Robin certainly was the name for her."

Mommy named me Elizabeth——after John the Baptist's mother——and Robin, after a pretty little Chinese singer they met once, and when I was born the little Chinese girl was so pleased that she sent me the sweetest little Chinese pajamas and slippers. Too bad we never met.

Speaking of that name, Robin, and birds...whenever I heard bright and sparkling music, like birds singing, I would forget myself and try to fly! I missed my wings so much on earth, and I was so disappointed when I would flap my arms and get nowhere.

But it was good, even though I had no wings. Some of them didn't know how good it was. Mommy heard once that some doctor had said babies who came into the world in my condition should be lined up in a row and "machine gunned," because they were no good to themselves or to anybody else. Father, if that remark was really made, forgive him, for he knows not what he's saying. I wish he could meet You....

*B*efore Cau-Cau came back from her vacation, Mommy, Daddy, and Dusty took me back to see the San Francisco doctor. That trip was a "pistol," as Daddy says. Was there trouble!

They put me in a "lower berth," in my bedstrap, and Dusty was in the berth above me. Mommy slept in the bed right across from me, and Daddy was in the bunk above hers. I was pretty restless during the night, but as soon as I had my breakfast, things quieted down. Dusty and I had fun looking out of the window at northern California; his eyes were as big as saucers.

A minister friend of Daddy met us at the station, and he took Dusty off for a ride on the "cable cars," and they took me to the hotel. I didn't do so well—I was nervous, and the hotel noises and the taxicab horns kept me from sleeping, and I had another "spell." The night after we saw the doctor, I kept my parents up all night.

They took turns walking me up and down the room. Finally, Daddy lay down on his bed, exhausted; he put me on his chest and patted my back and sang to me and mumbled words, trying to comfort me. Early in the morning my temperature shot up, and they sent for the doctor; he gave me a shot of "penicillin" and something to put me to sleep.

On the train going home, Mommy was up seven times in the night. I was sure glad to get back to my own little bed in Encino. Mommy and Daddy were there, too; they were so quiet! The doctor told them that my "muscle tone" was better but that my heart was getting worse.

My muscles *were* stronger. I could turn over in my bed, and I could even get on my hands and knees and hold myself in a crawling position. I had eight big teeth and I could chew crackers, which I called "cack-cack." (You see, my tongue was under better control, too.)

I had always had trouble trying to hold up my milk bottle. It was so heavy. Mommy and Ginny got a little perfume bottle, sterilized it and put a nipple on it, and it was so light that I could hold it in my own hands and drain it dry. Of course, my bones were tiny and weak, and there was still that soft spot on my head, which hadn't quite closed. I was tired most of the time, and they had trouble waking me up after my naps in the afternoon. I weighed seventeen pounds, five ounces—not much for a baby nearly two years old!

Cau-Cau took a day a week off now (she needed it!), and on the days when Mommy was working, I was alone with Ginny and Dusty. We had a great time playing around on the floor of my house. Dusty would hide under my bed and tease me. He was my favorite; while I couldn't talk to him, we always sort of knew what we were *trying* to say to each other. There was kind of a spark between us, Father, if You know what I mean.

Mommy never forgot what they told her when I was born—that I couldn't live very long. She was so anxious to be with me during the time I was on earth that she refused to fly in airplanes on trips. She was afraid she might "crash," and from the day I was born she had not put her foot in a plane. You put her to quite a test with that flying business.

There were some big religious meetings being held down in Houston, Texas, and Mommy and Daddy were asked to come and speak. Daddy went, but Mommy was afraid—afraid to *fly*, and she had to fly to get there on time. She let Daddy go, and she tossed all night in her bed, and in her sleep she heard You asking her, "Which comes first—Robin or Me?" It was a hard decision to make.

In the morning, she leaped out of bed, called the airport and made a reservation, and went off to Houston. I think that was the greatest victory of all on my whole mission—helping Mommy conquer *fear*. She was never afraid to go where You sent her after that. She knew it was more important to tell the world about what You were doing for her and for me than to stay in my room night and day.

She flew down to Texas again, shortly after this, to see my grandfather, who was sick. While she was there, You did it again: You led her out to a babies' home called Hope Cottage, in Dallas, where You had little Mary waiting to take my place. Mommy saw Mary while she was walking around the cottage—a little black-eyed baby, with blacker hair, who raised herself up on her elbows and watched Mommy walk around the room. She never took her eyes off Mommy; it was as though she were saying to herself, "Well! At last you've come!" Mommy couldn't take her eyes off Mary, either. Mommy found out that Mary was part Choctaw Indian, and that struck a spark. Daddy was part Choctaw Indian, too!

Mommy came back and told Daddy she sure hoped that little baby would find a good home with somebody, and I almost laughed out loud. I knew all about the home she was going to find: it was part of the Plan.

Mary's with them now, Father. I wish I could go Down There again and visit them. I'd like to see Mommy happy again, like she was the day I got my first tooth. I think I'll send word down to them to change Mary's name to "Doe"; there's something Choctaw about "Doe."

Daddy said he knew Dusty would like having Mary— or Doe—around, because Dusty was getting tired of being the youngest in the family—of being "low man on the totem pole" in our family. It will be good for Dusty, all right. He is "all boy and full of vinegar," but he was kind and tender with Your Littlest Angel—meaning me. It was something just to watch him go out of his way, more and more, to help me.

I saw that thoughtfulness developing in all the children in "the house of Rogers." On my birthday, Dusty took one of his best toys and wrapped it up in nice tissue paper and gave it to me. Linda prayed for me. She said the grace at meals, and the grace always included something about me. The night I left to come back Up Here, Linda went to Mommy and said, "I prayed for Robin in church this morning," and that gave Mommy a great lift. And she was always praying for Nancy, too.

Take good care of Linda, won't you, Father? She's so unselfish; she wants to be a nurse when she grows up, so she can help people—people like me. Cheryl is sweet, too; she wants to be an actress, but Mommy wants her to be a good Christian first, and Mommy knows that being an actress is a dangerous business. There are so many pit-falls. But I think Cheryl will make it, all right. She's got what it takes—You.

I was sorry to leave them, as I watched them becoming more and more unselfish and doing more and more for people who were weaker than they were. We did quite a job on those children, Father; they learned a great lesson, and they'll never forget it.

*W*ell, we're getting near the end of my story.

Things began to happen fast. Mommy and Daddy had to go to New York to appear in a rodeo, and they dreaded that because it meant leaving me, and I was getting no better. Mommy was in such a troubled state of mind that she couldn't settle down to getting her songs ready for the show, and she kept worrying about me and about Cau-Cau, who was tired out. What should she do? Go to New York? Let Cau-Cau go and stay with me night and day herself? Or what?

Everybody was uneasy and restless. Cau-Cau worried over my failure to walk. She worked so hard with me, exercising my legs, and when the "orthopedic" man told her it would be at least six months before I could walk, she almost cried. Mommy decided Cau-Cau had had enough and that she should leave me for her own sake.

They both cried when Cau-Cau went away. Poor Cau-Cau kept rubbing my legs until the very day she left us. I wanted so to tell her never mind, that I would soon be using wings instead of my poor feet, but I couldn't. It was awful, Father, seeing her turn away from me for the last time, but I'm glad now that she went. That last night would have been just too hard for her.

The other children, all of a sudden, got the mumps— and so did I! One side of my face swelled up and then went down, and then the other side swelled up, much worse, and before anybody could do anything, the fever hit my brain.

Two doctors came and worked hard over me; they did their best, but of course it wasn't any good. Late Saturday afternoon they took my temperature; it was 106.

Mommy called in one of the doctors who had been in the hospital the day I was born, and he gave me medicine to kill the pain, and he told Mommy that I cried so because I had a terrific headache.

Mommy and Daddy walked up and down, up and down, outside my little house. Daddy said, "God will call her when He's ready. We've just *got* to trust Him." The doctor came out and told them that I might go in a matter of seconds now. My kind of heart gave no warning, and they must be ready....

He told Mommy that she and Daddy had done the right thing in keeping me at home, loving me like they had. His own wife was going to have a little baby soon, he said, and if it were a baby like me, he would do the same thing.

Babies like me must have left their mark on him, for he said something You must love, Father; he said that he was going to theological school to equip himself, spiritually, so that he could be of more help to the parents of other problem babies like me. We really helped him, didn't We? Being with me will make him a better doctor with every patient he has from now on! It's good *he* didn't want to "machine gun" me, like that other doctor!

Later Sunday afternoon, my fever was 108; the doctor told Mommy that I had "mumps encephalitis," and that it was a bad development. Only one child out of nine developed encephalitis, and it was very, very dangerous. He didn't have much hope that I'd recover from it.

Part of the time when I was conscious, I could see them dimly, all around me. Most of the time I was reaching up for Your arms, Father, for I knew You were very near now. I knew You were coming.

Mommy came in and kissed my hand, and she noticed the funny, rattling way I was breathing; she looked grief-stricken, but there was a sort of peace on her face when she turned and went out on the porch.

My special pal, the dog, Lana, was out there. She kept walking up and down, up and down, restlessly, and then she began to bark, loud and insistently. Lana knew! Mommy patted her while she prayed a prayer of thanksgiving to You for letting me stay two years. Just as Daddy met her on the porch and she went crying into his arms, You came, and I felt myself being lifted up.

What a moment that was! Everything was bright with light, there was a sound like the rustling of a million angels' wings, and there was singing everywhere. My old clay shell just fell off, my heart began beating strong and steady, and my head didn't hurt anymore.

*W*ell, that's it, Father. That's what happened Down There. That's how I delivered Your message, and I'm sure they got it. They learned, for one thing, that there are many mansions, or "rooms," in Your earthly house—that there's a room for the strong and a room for the sick, a room for the healthy and a room for the weak, a room for those born with ten talents and a room for those with only one, a room for the rich and a room for the poor. A room for *everyone* and something for them to do in that room for You. In Your house Down There are many rooms, where we study and teach and get ready to move into Your big light room Up Here.

We did pretty well in that room in my little house, Father. We taught them to see purpose in pain and messages on the crosses they have to carry around. You know, when Daddy sings now in his big rodeo show, he has a lot of spotlights making a cross in the center of the arena. It's sort of a symbol of what's happened to him and to Mommy: the cross has become the great big thing in the middle of their lives. Everything else in their lives now sort of moves around it, like a wheel around a hub.

They're a lot stronger since they got Our message. There's a new glory inside them and on everything all around them, and they've made up their minds to give it to everybody they meet. The sun's a lot brighter in Encino since we stopped off there for a while.

And now, Father, please…could I just go out and try my wings?

Say Yes to Tomorrow

DALE EVANS ROGERS

with Floyd W. Thatcher

Contents

A Personal Word
TO OUR READERS

On a calendar that graces the Rogers's kitchen are these words by an anonymous author:

Take time to think, it is the source of power.
Take time to read, it is the foundation of wisdom.
Take time to play, it is the secret of staying young.
Take time to be quiet, it is the opportunity to seek God.
Take time to be aware, it is the opportunity to help others.
Take time to love and be loved, it is God's greatest gift.
Take time to laugh, it is the music of the soul.
Take time to be friendly, it is the road to happiness.
Take time to dream, it is what the future is made of.
Take time to pray, it is the greatest power on earth.

As we have looked up at these words day after day, the wisdom of this unknown author has expressed our deepest feelings. Let's face it—sometimes in today's world it is hard to say *Yes* to God for our todays and our tomorrows and for all that comes our way.

When we listen to the evening news at six and ten and hear all of the bad things that have happened, it is easy to become depressed and think that God has given up on us and our world. And the daily newspapers—even the so-called comic sections—don't make it any easier to believe anything good ever happens.

For example, in November 1992 a news item datelined Atlantic City, New Jersey, carried the headline: "Unattended Kids a Problem in Casinos." The lead line read, "Melissa leans against a casino wall, looking crumpled, tired and scared. She is nine years old." The writer then briefly describes the scene. It is midnight, and Melissa is waiting for her mother to finish a gambling spree. A security guard has been keeping an eye on her for two hours while trying to locate her mother. "My mother's in there and I want her," the little girl says, her brown eyes welling with tears. "I want to go to our room."

And just a month later, the newspapers released the story of a couple who had gone to Mexico on a vacation for over a week and had left their two little girls—nine and four years old—home alone to shift for themselves.

Yes, it seems that all news worth printing is bad news.

Children are neglected and abused, car thefts have reached an all-time high, and in many places it isn't safe to walk the neighborhood after dark. But the message we need to hear loud and clear is this, "God is still in charge!" Our world has been beset with evil since the beginning of time, but as Christians, we know that with the death and resurrection of our Lord the battle against the bad news of sin and evil has been won for all time.

With Christ in charge of our lives, we can say *Yes* to today and *Yes* to tomorrow. And we can say *Yes* to all of God's wonderful gifts. The apostle Paul beautifully expressed who and what we are:

> *In all these things we are more than conquerors*
> *through him who loved us, [and we are] convinced*
> *that neither death, nor life, nor angels, nor rulers, nor*
> *things present, nor things to come, nor powers, nor*
> *height, nor depth, nor anything else in all creation,*
> *will be able to separate us from the love of God in*
> *Christ Jesus our Lord.*

[Rom. 8:37-39]

With promises such as this, you and I *can* make a difference! God's provisions and gifts for a rich, full, and rewarding life are ours. Now, let's accept and use those gifts to make this a better world—a place where God's love is clearly seen and felt.

Yes, puzzling things happen to Christians—death takes loved ones; people disappoint us; we are hurt and suffer reverses. But we can say *Yes* to all of our tomorrows and move ahead boldly and with confidence because of these electrically charged words of Jesus, "In the world you will have trouble. But courage! The victory is mine; I have conquered the world" (John 16:33 NEB).

1

Say Yes to
GOD'S GIFT OF TOMORROW

For yesterday is but a dream,
And tomorrow is only a vision;
But today well lived makes every
yesterday a dream of happiness,
And every tomorrow a vision of hope.

*I*t was New Year's Eve, and the temperature hovered at forty-two degrees below zero. Eighteen thousand United States Marines were poised for battle on the front lines in Korea opposite one hundred thousand hardened and fanatic Communist troops.

At midnight the Marines celebrated the New Year by dining on a ration of cold beans scooped out of tin cans while standing alongside their tanks. One of the newspaper correspondents attached to this advance unit observed a big, burly Marine, his clothing and beard frozen stiff, eating his beans with a trench knife.

Sidling up to the stoic Marine, the newspaper correspondent asked, "If I were God and could give you one thing you'd rather have than anything else in the world, what would you ask for?"

After a few thoughtful moments and with no noticeable change of expression, the Marine answered, "I would ask you to give me tomorrow."[1]

That stark Korean scene reminded us of another army that over three thousand years ago was camped along the eastern banks of the Jordan River on the level expanse of the Plains of Moab. Across the rapidly flowing river was a formidable foe that was firmly ensconced within walled fortifications that had withstood bandit attacks and invading armies for centuries.

While we don't have a first-person report by trained observers, it is not hard to imagine the mood of the people in that Israelite camp. For long, hot, weary, and dreary years they had bivouacked in the lonely stretches of the vast Sinai wilderness because their fathers and grandfathers had refused to obey the Lord and by faith occupy the land promised long before to their ancestors. The years since their stubborn decision had been bitter times of pain, heartache, and waiting. But they had learned their lesson, and God had given them a second chance. The cloud by day and the pillar of fire by night had guided them in the Sinai and north past Mount Hor to their point of entry to their Promised Land across the Jordan and opposite the ancient city of Jericho.

We don't know the precise route they took, but we do know that it stretched out to approximately one hundred miles of rugged country and mountainous terrain. It was a hot, dusty, and perilous trip with hostile peoples along the way. It had to have been a relief to pitch their camp in sight of Jericho and Canaan even though they knew their future would be full of the unknown and obvious danger.

It doesn't take much imagination to picture what was probably going on in the mind of the commanding general of those Israelite forces. Although well past mid-life and advancing rapidly into that stage irreverently called "old age," Joshua doubtless carried a vivid picture of that scene more than forty years before when he and Caleb risked their lives for what they believed to be the truth, in obedience to the Lord's instructions. After spying out the land, ten of their compatriot covert agents pessimistically insisted that the Israelites were no match for their Canaanite enemies— to invade Canaan would be suicide, God's instructions and promises to the contrary. Only Joshua and Caleb spoke firmly in favor of launching the invasion. It was a bitter moment when the other ten spies had their way.

And I'm sure it wasn't hard for Joshua to relive the scene in which an unruly mob threatened to kill him and Caleb simply because they advocated doing what God had told them to do. Yes, those had been long and lonely years, but now—tomorrow—they were to break camp, cross the Jordan River, and move into their long-promised land that flowed "with milk and honey."

Joshua could at that moment say *Yes* to his tomorrow with all of its unknowns because God had assured him that he would be with his people and they would succeed. The days, months, and years of lonely waiting would soon be history. At the same time, Joshua undoubtedly remembered the details of the majority report of the other ten spies even though forty years had dragged by since that infamous day. The report pictured the Canaanites as a formidable foe, and their heavily fortified, walled cities would be impossible to take. The report had insisted that there was no way the Israelite army could subdue the giants who would be arrayed against them. And by comparison they saw themselves as mere grasshoppers.

But things were different now. Even with the waters of the Jordan at flood stage, they could say *Yes* to their tomorrow in confidence that God would see them across that barrier because he had promised to be with them. It was this same God who had engineered the escape of their fathers and grandfathers from Egyptian slavery. It was he who had guided them across the Sinai wilderness in safety to the sacred mountain where many years before Moses had been confronted by God in the burning bush. And it was God who, in spite of their bouts of rancorous disobedience, hadn't given up on them and would now—tomorrow—escort them into their Promised Land. What a glad day that would be!

Believe me, as I have moved into those years beyond the time known as mid-life, I somehow find it easy to identify with that cold Marine in Korea as he looked out across the shell-pocked no-man's-land and with General Joshua as he stared at the distant palm trees on the western side of the Jordan. There may be much about what is going on around us that is discouraging and seems impossible to handle, but ours is a God of the impossible. I am confident that as we place our faith in him, he will see us not only through today but through all of our tomorrows as well.

At the same time, though, I must confess to being puzzled by the depressingly negative attitudes that seem to plague so many people today—even Christians. It appears to be increasingly popular to concentrate on the dark side of life, to hang crepe and moan about everything that is wrong with the world. It is true that much of what dominates our news is horribly depressing—inner-city riots, looting, child abuse, abuse of the aged, scenes of hunger and starvation in third-world countries, and senseless violence.

All of this, accompanied by the carping diatribes of the noisiest of our politicians, is almost enough to plunge any sane person into the black abyss of gloom. Certainly, there is no denying the agonizing difficulties that plague us all from time to time. Yes, there is evil in our world, but to stop there, I believe, is to leave God entirely out of our calculations.

It is likely in the midst of all this that you have discovered, as I have, that present in every crowd are those who parrot the hackneyed notion that life was better and sweeter "in the good old days." It's strange that as we grow older we tend to glorify the past as we remember it. That old nostalgia virus seems to be highly contagious. I'm sure most of us can at times identify with a humorist, whose name escapes me, when he said, "Nostalgia is like a grammar lesson: we find the present *tense* and the past *perfect*."

In our better and more thoughtful moments we know beyond all doubt that though the past is terribly important, it most certainly was not *perfect*. And, yes, memory is essential to our health and wholeness, but that is just one side of the coin. The apostle Paul spoke to the other side when he urged his Christian friends in the Roman colony of Philippi in northern Greece to put the past behind and stretch or strain forward toward life ahead. I believe this was his way of telling them and us that even though our world may seem askew at times, we can say *Yes* to tomorrow with confidence that God will be with us at all times.

The late Dr. Paul Tournier, noted Swiss psychiatrist, gave us this profound insight in one of his lectures, "Life is not a stable state, but a rhythm, an alternation, a succession of new births."[2] Indeed, for the person whose faith is firmly anchored in the Lord, every tomorrow offers the opportunity for "a succession of new births." And for the Christian there is no room in this rhythm of tomorrows for the depressing gray and black clouds of doom, gloom, and pessimism.

Without a doubt, one of the most influential persons in my own Christian pilgrimage is Dr. Norman Vincent Peale, who for many years was the senior minister of New York's historic Marble Collegiate Church and who, even as I write this, is celebrating his ninety-fourth birthday. In one of Dr. Peale's sermons he speaks of Jesus Christ being "as fresh as tomorrow morning's newspaper. He is everlastingly new and gives us newness of life." For Dr. Peale "Christianity is the religion of the new." Then he adds that as we follow Christ and the advice the apostle Paul gave his Philippian friends, "We will stop saying gloomily that things are getting bad and that we haven't seen the worst," and we will come to see that "Christianity is the religion of the getting better."[3]

That kind of talk rings the bell! After all, as Christians we have a long and rich heritage. Our God is indeed the Creator and Sustainer of our vast universe and everything and everyone in it. As a matter of fact, the writer of the Gospel of Matthew gives us the marvelous assurance that our heavenly Father knows each of us intimately and values us greatly. And with this kind of Good News tucked safely into our awareness, we have no cause for dismal pessimism and, certainly, no reason to be concerned about our tomorrows. Instead, we can claim the future with pragmatic and hardheaded optimism because *God is in charge!*

Many years ago at a retreat for the Hollywood Christian Group at Forest Home Conference Grounds high in the San Bernardino Mountains of southern California, our mentor, Dr. Richard C. Halverson, who was at the time the Associate Minister of the First Presbyterian Church of Hollywood, encouraged and urged us to keep on keeping on in our Christian walk and witness in spite of the temptations that confronted all of us as professional actors and entertainers in the Hollywood scene. Then, as now, we were faced with the moral, economic, and spiritual crises that plague and threaten our society. Dick urged us to be mindful daily that Jesus Christ is the Captain of our faith and the Source of our serenity, strength, and hope. And even now as I'm reminded of that particular event, those times, and Dick's counsel, I find it very reassuring that he is taking that same message into the hallowed halls of the United States Senate in Washington as he ministers to our nation's political leadership in his role of senate chaplain.

So as we persist in our faith during all of our todays and claim with confidence our tomorrows for God, we know that there is no stage in life when we are free to coast or drift. This is most definitely not an option for us as everyday Christians whether we're in our twenties, our forties, or our eighties.

Dr. Frank C. Laubach was a great Christian hero of a generation ago. Dr. Frank spent his life as a missionary and literacy expert. He and his associates were instrumental in opening the door to a new life by teaching thousands of people to read who otherwise would never have had a chance. He was also a gifted translator, and I like the way he translated those wonderful words of the apostle Paul found in his perceptive letter written to the Christians in the Roman province of Galatia. This is the way it reads, "So let us not grow tired of doing good. When the time comes, if we do not lose heart, we shall gather a good harvest." And Paul's next words seem to speak incisively to late twentieth-century Christians of all persuasions, "So let us do good to all men [people] whenever we have a chance. *Let us do good especially to those who belong to the family of our Christian faith.*"[4] There is just no room in those words for the kind of judgmental bickering and pharisaical criticism of our fellow Christians that we sometimes hear and see in the press and on television.

My spirits have always been buoyed up and made to soar by the words of the ancient psalmist, who in a moment of noble inspiration—possibly after absorbing the exquisite beauty of the scarlet and gold eastern sky at sunrise—gave us this positive affirmation,

This is the day of the Lord's victory; let us be happy,
let us celebrate!

[Ps. 118:24 TEV]

Yes, our todays and tomorrows are meant for celebration —they are God's special gifts to us and are ours to use creatively as we live for the Lord and for his people wherever they are in today's world.

There is a little stone plaque hanging in our kitchen that was sent to us by our dear friend Dr. Lloyd Ogilvie, insightful writer of many wonderful books and the gifted preacher on the "Let God Love You" television program. The plaque reads, "Living each day as if it were our only day makes for a total life lived at full potential." Each time I read this sagacious message I am reminded that my goal as a Christian is to live every tomorrow at full potential. And I'm also reminded that while I can't do this on my own, I have a heavenly Father who is in charge of my every tomorrow.

In a moment of high inspiration the writer of Isaiah assured his readers through all time that

Those who hope in the LORD will renew their
strength.
They will soar on wings like eagles; they will run and
not grow weary, they will walk and not be faint.

[Isa. 40:31 NIV]

It seems to me that as we make our way through these exciting and eventful years that close out the twentieth century and prepare for the wonders God has for us in the twenty-first, we will find it inspiring to tap the wisdom of another psalm writer who thousands of years ago wrote,

> *Great is the LORD, and greatly to be praised;*
> *his greatness is unsearchable [beyond our ability*
> *to understand].*
> *The LORD is gracious and merciful, slow to anger*
> *and abounding in steadfast love.*
> *The LORD is good to all, and his compassion is over*
> *all that he has made.*
>
> [Ps. 145:3, 8–9]

Over and over again the writers of the Psalms express profound confidence in the unfailing goodness of the Lord and assure us that we can trust him implicitly not only for our todays but for our tomorrows as well. Admittedly, in our hurry and rush and frantic striving to make some sort of sense out of today's high-tech and computerized world, it is easy to lose touch with the kind of a God whom the psalmist knew and felt in their pastoral environment. There is so much about modern life with its hustle and bustle that tends to rob us of that intimate sense of God's presence. Consequently, it seems that all too often we find it easy to forget that God does indeed feel compassion for everything and everyone he has made. Unlike what happens so often with modern computers, God is never "down"; he is always there!

In reflecting further on these words from the psalmist, another scene comes to mind in which Jesus was looking out across the hills and valleys of Galilee, and his eyes apparently took in the vast panorama of vineyards and grain fields in which flocks of colorful birds were feeding. The scene inspired Jesus to say, "Look at the birds of the air; they neither sow nor reap nor gather into barns, and yet your heavenly Father feeds them." And then he added, "Consider the lilies of the field, how they grow; they neither toil nor spin"—and yet God cares for them (Matt. 6:26, 28).

A spectacular illustration of God's meticulous care can be seen each winter along the colorful coast of central California just a couple of hundred miles north and west of our home in the high desert. Each year in early October the large, colorful, orange and black Monarch butterflies begin to arrive and cluster on the eucalyptus and Monterey pine trees near the little resort community of Pismo Beach—the terminus of their migration from points as far away as Canada.

As the chill of winter envelops their habitat in the faraway north country, these little creatures with a wingspread of not more than four inches make their way south and west at speeds of up to thirty miles an hour. And after crossing the heights of the Rocky Mountains and the Sierra Nevadas, they continue on west to the California coast and settle, layer upon layer, on the leaves and branches of the eucalyptuses and pines.

The thousands upon thousands of orange and black Monarchs transform those trees into colorful and fluttering masses of wings. Tourists and nature lovers flock to this sensational scene and watch in wonder by the hour. Then in late February the little Monarchs begin to leave their central California sanctuaries and head east and north to their homes in the far north, somehow sensing the arrival there of spring and warm weather.

Is all of this just an accident of nature? I don't think so for one minute. Rather, I believe that these delicate little creatures are guided through their life span by a loving God who has created in them the instinct to make their annual migration south and west...and then months later east and north.

For me, the sight of these Monarchs is just one among many such illustrations of the loving care of our Creator-God for us and for this world of ours. With this kind of a God we can most certainly say *Yes* not only to today but to all our tomorrows with calm confidence. With the apostle Paul we can draw on this eternal truth and begin each day with perhaps the most astounding and life-changing affirmation of all time, "I can do all things through him [Christ] who strengthens me" (Phil. 4:13).

The American Southwest provided the stage for a rugged and stalwart people during the raw and turbulent days of the nineteenth century. Among the most heroic of them was Juan Bautista Lamy, a missionary priest who in 1851 was assigned as bishop to this desert diocese with headquarters in Santa Fe. This zealous and erudite missionary bishop made a profound spiritual impact on people from the Rocky Mountains across Colorado, New Mexico, Arizona, and into old Mexico. In 1875 Lamy was elevated to archbishop. From then until his death in 1884 Bishop Lamy continued to exercise valiant and heroic influence throughout the arid vastness of the southwestern frontier. His entire career was carved out of great hardship. But Paul Horgan, the author of *Lamy of Santa Fe*, captured the vitality of this rugged and noble man when he wrote that each day Bishop Lamy "awoke a new man." Certainly Bishop Lamy was a man of his day—and of his tomorrow.

Author Henri Nouwen expressed the idea of Christian expectation in this brief sentence from his book entitled *The Genesee Diary*, "An important part of the spiritual life is to keep longing, waiting, hoping, expecting." These words are a modern extension of the apostle Paul's thinking when he wrote,

> *This one thing I do: forgetting what lies behind and straining forward to what lies ahead, I press on*

toward the goal for the prize of the heavenly call of
God in Christ Jesus.

[Phil. 3:13–14]

And in this pressing on process it comes through loud and clear that Paul lived each day in a way that would make Christ and the Christian faith attractive.

In a little book published many years ago by Grace Cathedral in San Francisco, an unnamed writer left behind this prayer:

Let me be so strong that nothing can disturb my
peace of mind.
Let me look on the sunny side of everything and
make my optimism come true.
Let me be just as enthusiastic about the success of
others as I am about my own...
Let me wear a cheerful countenance at all times,
and have a smile ready for every living creature
I meet...
Let me be too large for worry, too noble for anger,
too strong for fear and too happy to permit the
presence of trouble.[5]

And to that prayer I would add this last sentence,

Lord, let me always say **Yes** *to tomorrow.*

Say Yes to
GOD'S GIFT OF CHANGE AND GROWTH

If we don't change, we don't grow.
If we don't grow, we are not really living.

Gail Sheehy

If we all just kept on doing exactly what we've done
up to now, most people would never change, and
people are changing all the time. That's what growth
is: doing things you've never done before, sometimes
things you once didn't even dream you could.

Mildred Newman and Bernard Berkswitz

*W*hen Booth Tarkington, twice a winner of the Pulitzer prize and author of some forty novels, was seventy-five years old, someone asked him whether older people felt old in spirit. His reply was a classic, "I don't know. Why don't you ask someone who is old?"

Born in 1869, just four years after the close of the tragic American Civil War, Mr. Tarkington grew up and grew older during years of expeditious change and expansive growth in American life. And by the time of his death in 1946, he had witnessed revolutionary transformations—in transportation from bulky horse and wagon to sleek aircraft; in communication from Pony Express to radio and the promise of television. In this interval the United States had become densely populated and economically energetic from the rugged shores of the Atlantic Coast on the east to the placid Pacific in the far west. These were exhilarating times in the life of our country—years of radical change and explosive growth. But for a person like Booth Tarkington, change and growth fired his imagination and kept him ever young in spite of the passing years.

In our better and more thoughtful moments, we all know that the comforts and ease of the lifestyle we enjoy now in these closing years of the twentieth century came to us as a result of the restless refusal of our fathers, mothers, grandfathers, and grandmothers to be satisfied with the existing state of affairs. It was the insatiable thirst for the new that forced open the way for change and progress. And it is this same spirit that has unveiled a whole new universe for us as men, women, and machines have penetrated the mysterious outer reaches of limitless space.

Yet there is a strange phenomenon at work within each of us that stubbornly resists change and clings tenaciously to comfortable old ideas and things that remain exactly as they are. With our heads we may accept the idea expressed some twenty-five hundred years ago by Heracleitus of Ephesus who taught that "everything is flowing" and pointed out that a person cannot step twice into the same river because every moment the water changes. But with our hearts we don't want the waters of our lives to be disturbed or changed. For most of us, change for any reason is to be avoided like a cloud of pesky mosquitoes. We resist change with all of the strength we can muster. A friend of ours keeps a little plaque above his desk that reads, "As long as you don't change anything...I'm flexible." Sounds strangely familiar, doesn't it?

Our friend Bruce Larson, talented writer and preacher, understood well the human tendency when he wrote,

Even the most adventuresome of us—those of us who are the least committed to and defensive of the past—still fear change. I've read that people who have been faced with freezing to death in the snow experience a cozy warm feeling that seduces them into inactivity. To stay alive during long exposure to freezing conditions, one has to go against instinctive feelings. To think the way we always have, to act in

> *old patterns is non-threatening and comfortable, but it lulls us toward a frightening death of the soul. To stay alive we must be people on the move, alert to the exciting opportunities of change.*[1]

Bruce Larson has expressed a truth that rings true. It is dreadfully easy for most of us to "act in old patterns," to become comfortable with things as they are. Michael Marshall, gifted author and eminent churchman, writes along this line: "There is a warmth and security in the old and the known and the tried ways of life. Part of the power of nostalgia is that it makes no demands upon us to go outside the territory with which we are already familiar."[2]

But if we are to stay alive to the possibilities God has for us, we must each day welcome change—the thinking of new thoughts and the doing of new things—that enables us to grow, develop, and mature in the Christian faith. In fact, "Faith and change are two sides of the same coin. Without faith we cannot change creatively. If we have no goals—no vision—no reason to believe in the future—we cannot create that future."[3]

Frankly, when I'm wrestling with an idea as unsettling as the importance of change in my life, I find it helpful to turn through the pages of my Bible for models among its many heroes and heroines. Again and again in such excursions a moral and spiritual—yet very human—giant moves off the page and onto the center stage of my imagination.

His name is Moses.

I won't review here the details of Moses' early life as a child and young adult—years spent as a prince and likely as a scribe in the top levels of sophisticated Egyptian royalty and society. Instead, I'll pick up on the story at the stage of Moses' life when he was somewhere between forty and fifty years of age.

Because of a cataclysmic series of events, Moses had abandoned everything familiar to him and had traveled several hundred miles east and south of his home in Egypt to what is described as "the land of Midian." As were the Hebrews, the Midianites were descendants of Abraham. According to the ancient story, after Sarah died, Abraham married Keturah, and they had six sons—one of whom was named Midian. And evidently by the time of Moses at least some clans of the descendants of Midian lived on the east of the Gulf of Aqaba, one of the branches of the Red Sea.

Because of their common ancestry, Moses undoubtedly felt he would be well received and accepted by the Midianites. And he was. In fact, we're told, according to the Bible story, that Moses was accepted as a member of the household and clan of an important Midianite chieftain by the name of Jethro. And to further seal the relationship, Moses married one of Jethro's daughters and they had two sons.

Now, while the Midianites were a nomadic people,

their culture was quite sophisticated. For example, we know that they were proficient in metal work and that the people of the Kenite clan, to which Jethro belonged, were especially skilled in the metal-working art. They were, in fact, known as the coppersmiths of the desert. All of this is simply to say that Moses with his advanced Egyptian education had every reason to feel at home and comfortable with his adopted Midianite country-people.

And feel at home he did, because he spent many years in Midian. In addition, it is apparent that as the son-in-law of the wealthy and influential Jethro, Moses assumed important and responsible tribal duties and was in charge of at least a sizable portion of his father-in-law's herds of sheep and cattle. It is quite likely, too, that with the passing of the years—just how many we do not know—as Moses managed Jethro's vast herds, he became familiar not only with the immediate environs of Midian but also with at least some portions of the vast Sinai Peninsula a hundred miles or so from Jethro's encampment.

In fact, it was at Mount Horeb (Sinai), probably well over a hundred miles from the comfort and security of his home and Jethro's headquarters that Moses had his encounter with God in the drama of the burning bush, which the Exodus writer reported in vivid detail. The landscape was doubtless familiar to Moses and his men. And it wasn't a particularly unusual sight to see a thorn-bush on fire, because the intense desert heat would often cause a dry and brittle bush to burst into flame. This time something was different. Moses was startled because the bush was not only on fire, but it was not burning up and disintegrating.

You remember the story, I'm sure, but briefly, when Moses' curiosity edged him up to this phenomenon, he immediately learned that he was on sacred ground for out of the bush came the voice of God. And equally frightening, the message was intensely disturbing. After identifying himself and bringing to mind the plight of the Hebrews in Egypt, God said, "I will send you to Pharaoh to bring my people, the Israelites, out of Egypt" (Exod. 3:10).

For Moses this was a most distressing message, and according to the story he put up quite an argument. After all, he had escaped from Egypt many years before as a hunted fugitive. It would be suicide to go back there, and besides, who would believe him? And in addition to all of that, he protested, "I have never been eloquent...I am slow of speech and slow of tongue" (Exod. 4:10). But God was persistent, and while going back to Egypt was a terrifying prospect, Moses knew what he had to do.

We have no way of knowing what went on in Moses' mind as he trudged the many miles from the slopes of Mount Horeb north and around the narrow branch of the Red Sea and then south to Jethro's encampment. Surely wild and bizarre thoughts must have raced through his mind. And we just have to believe that during those long and lonely hours, he was reminded again and again of the comfort and security of his pleasant life with his family and friends; it was ridiculous to leave everything he had come to know and love behind! And yet, according to the story, when Moses arrived back at the tent of his father-in-law, he said, "Please let me go back to my kindred in Egypt" (Exod. 4:18).

Next, as the adventure unfolds, we find Moses on his way back to Egypt to fulfill his destiny. It had to be an agonizing time in many ways for him as he confronted the uncertainty of the future. As the Bible drama plays out, we catch the scenes of Moses standing up against Egypt's Pharaoh and ultimately, with God's help, leading the Israelites out of their slavery across the arid wilderness to the very mountain where he had had his burning-bush encounter with God. No longer tongue-tied and fearful, he was now a political and military leader of his people. And it was at Sinai that he assumed the role of spiritual leader of Israel and received the living words of the Ten Commandments from God on the mountain summit above the clouds.

Yes, Moses must have had to struggle bitterly with the agony of change and the risk it involved. In the process he grew to become the man who justly merited the accolade of the Deuteronomy writer, "Never since has there arisen a prophet in Israel like Moses, whom the LORD knew face to face" (Deut. 34:10).

As we reflect on the Moses saga and the model he has given us for saying *Yes* to change and growth, we become increasingly aware of the fact that this is both a rewarding and at the same time painful experience because it frequently means separating ourselves from the known and the familiar. Yet it can be a rewarding time as we respond to God's guidance.

One further thought before we leave the Moses story. While the chronology cannot be exact, Moses' dramatic change likely took place when he was well past the allotted three score and ten. This is an important thought because it underscores the fact that we never grow too old to change.

Saying *Yes* to change and growth means that at every stage and age we are living beyond the usual boundaries of life. In his book *Learn to Grow Old*, Dr. Paul Tournier reminds us of these important words of General Douglas MacArthur, who in 1945 at the age of sixty-five said, "You don't grow old from living a particular number of years; you get old because you have deserted your ideals. Years wrinkle your skin; renouncing your ideals wrinkles your soul. Worry, doubt, fear, and despair are the enemies which slowly bring us down to the ground and turn us to dust before we die."[4]

Wrinkled souls filled with worry, doubt, fear, and despair—such a description goes against everything God intends for us as people created in the image of God.

Instead, as children of the King, each new day is meant to be lived in a spirit of anticipation and excitement. Most certainly, a gloom and doom attitude is anti-Christian—it goes against everything Jesus modeled for us in his life, death, and resurrection.

In the last few years I have become increasingly aware that our late twentieth century world is plagued by a dull and lackluster sameness. Cities, towns, neighborhoods, houses, fenced yards, and, yes, people, all take on a sort of flat, dull sameness, almost as if they were stamped out by a cosmic cookie cutter. It seems that many people suffer from an overdose of humdrum. Every day is the same—work, eat, watch television, and sleep. Can it be that we have become prisoners of the way things are?

Even many Christians seem to have become victims of the dullness virus, and we've become dyspeptic and even belligerent when confronted with new ideas, with new expressions, and by people who obviously do not wear our particular label. We resist having our little boats rocked by any wave of change. Our values and attitudes have become calcified, and we refuse to let our dull and comfortable routines be challenged or disturbed in any way.

A generation ago Dorothy Sayers, an exceptionally talented British Christian and writer, recognized the truth of this when she wrote, "Somehow or other, and with the best of intentions, we have shown the world the typical Christian in the likeness of a crashing bore—and this in the name of One who assuredly never bored a soul in those thirty-three years during which he passed through the world like a flame."[5]

Indeed the Gospel writers give us a picture of a Jesus who was attractive to the crowds of ordinary people who dogged his footsteps and made him a welcome guest at parties and celebrations. It is interesting, isn't it, that his first recorded public appearance after his baptism was at a wedding celebration in the little community of Cana in Galilee. No, there wasn't anything dull and boring about this Jesus whose mission was to make all things new and to plant the seeds of change and growth.

And there was nothing dull and commonplace about the people who appear on the pages of our New Testament drama. In fact, early Christianity was a vibrant and explosive force that worked exciting change throughout all of the Mediterranean world during the first century. Life for them was full of novelty and spontaneity. There was an attractive effervescence about them that shouted *Yes* to life. They were not *trying* to change; it just happened, and their joy and vitality was instantly contagious.

One of my twentieth-century spiritual heroines is Mrs. Charles E. Cowman, the author and compiler of several best-selling devotional books that have nourished my soul for many years. On one occasion she wrote, "Somewhere near the snowy summit of the Alps there is an inscription that marks the last resting place of an

Alpine guide. Just three short words tell the story, 'He died climbing.' We often hear it said that 'so and so is growing old.' But we don't *grow* old. We only *get* old when we cease to grow and climb."

It is interesting, though, that as we grow and climb, the panorama of our lives changes constantly. The terrain doesn't necessarily become easier or more level, but as our perspective changes and matures, we are better able to confront life's challenges with the same kind of zest that characterized those early New Testament Christians. Somewhere among his prolific writings Dr. B. F. Skinner, insightful interpreter of human nature, observed, "Older people who see themselves as doing useful and interesting things fare better in every way than ones who merely take it easy."

Another gifted writer, Evelyn Underhill, underlines this same idea, "To be spiritually alive means to be growing and changing; not to settle down among a series of systemized beliefs and duties, but to endure and go on enduring the strains, conflicts and difficulties incident to development."[6]

"Be spiritually alive"—yes, that is the goal for each of us. And, yes, this calls for us to be open to change as we move through the various stages of life. From change comes new growth and the doing of new things. In fact, I have slowly come to see that this is the keynote in our Christian pilgrimage. I like the way an old friend has translated what the apostle Paul had to say about newness when he wrote these words to his friends in the bustling city of Corinth, "From this time on, then, let us look at others not with our limited human insight. Although we have perceived Christ humanly, let us no longer look at him that way." Because, "if any person has been joined with Christ...*he or she is a new person*; the old way of looking at life has passed away, and from this new perspective *everything has become fresh and new.*"[7]

I have often been challenged by an exchange between the gifted poet and writer of past years, Henry Wadsworth Longfellow, and a friend and admirer of his. While the two were visiting one day, the friend noted Longfellow's cotton white hair, which was in vivid contrast to his ruddy complexion and animated spirit. Knowing that the poet was well along in years, his friend asked how he was able to remain so alive and vigorous and to write so beautifully.

In reply Longfellow pointed to an apple tree nearby that was loaded with brilliantly colored blossoms. "That apple tree," he said, "is very old, but I never saw prettier blossoms upon it than those it now bears. The tree grows a little new wood each year, and I suppose it is out of the new wood that these blossoms come. Like the apple tree I try to grow a little new wood each year."

"A little new wood each year"—that is to be our goal as followers of the New Way and as citizens of Jesus' New

Society. This is the recipe for colorful change and growth. And as I reflect on my life—from the rural cotton town of Italy, Texas, to Hollywood, and in later years to the California high desert community of Victorville where we established the Roy Rogers–Dale Evans Museum—I am amazed at the "new wood." There have been times of effervescent joy and hours of searing heartbreak. Yet like the kaleidoscope I loved as a child, with each movement the scene changes and the sparkling combinations of color are more beautiful.

Little by little I have come to see that it is movement and change that bring spice and drama into our lives at whatever age and stage we are, especially as we move into mid-life and beyond. In reality, mid-life and the later mature years are times "for discovery, not stagnation." These are times "ripe for fresh beginnings.... If approached with good humor, flexibility, and an openness to change, the middle years and beyond can be the best half of life."[8] Yes, it is in the doing of new things in a planned and calculated way that we find the inspiration to cast off our prefabricated prejudices and assembly-line attitudes.

Samuel H. Miller was a warm and devoted Christian of a generation or two ago. He acquired a world of wisdom as the pastor of Old Cambridge Baptist Church and Dean of Harvard Divinity School, but his little book entitled *The Life of the Soul* may well be his greatest legacy. In it Dr. Miller issues this challenge, "The only way in which we can grow into something better than we are now is to do things we're not strictly able to do. We will have to subject ourselves to certain disciplines, the practice of exercises which we will not do well at first, and will take a great deal of failing before we accomplish the satisfactions of a skillful soul."[9]

It was this spirit that motivated another Old Testament hero of mine. Undoubtedly, everything in the Sumerian city of Ur of the Chaldeans was familiar and quite predictable to Abraham. But the biblical narrative tells us that he and his family left Ur and traveled north to Haran, a stopping point on the way to Canaan, the final destination. And next we read that after staying in Haran for a time the Lord said to Abraham, "Go from your country and your kindred and your father's house to the land that I will show you" (Gen. 12:1). It must have been a frightening thing for seventy-five-year-old Abraham to move out from the familiar and the known to the unfamiliar and the unknown, but he did. And for Abraham, life began at seventy-five because by faith Abraham obeyed God as he set out, not knowing where he was going. Imagine! That is *change* in capital letters.

Here is the secret. It is *by faith* that we can say *Yes* to all of tomorrow's change and growth. And as we move out in faith, we may not know exactly where we are going any more than Abraham did, but the same Lord who guided him each plodding step to his Promised Land will guide us. It is true we will not know the how, where, and when of God's leading, and at time the route and the timing may seem puzzling, but we can take comfort in the confidence that wherever we are, Christ has been there ahead of us.

You remember that when Joshua and the people of Israel were poised on the east bank of the Jordan River at flood stage opposite the city of Jericho they had no set of detailed instructions and no road map. All they had was God's promise, "I will be with you," and the priests carrying the ark of the covenant were told to move forward and step into the water. And it wasn't until they got their feet wet that a miracle happened—the way across was clear and they could proceed to their tomorrow.

3

Say Yes to
GOD'S GIFT OF JOY
AND LAUGHTER

Joy to the world! the Lord is come;
Let earth receive her King;
Let every heart prepare Him room,
And heaven and nature sing.

Joy to the world! the Savior reigns;
Let men their songs employ;
While fields and floods, rocks, hills and plains,
Repeat the sounding joy.

Isaac Watts

*I*n a letter from Parson John to Miriam Gray come these pearls of wisdom:

> *Many of the religious people that I know, when they*
> *talk of religion, have a bedside manner and walk*
> *about in felt slippers. And if they speak of God they*
> *always tidy themselves first. But you go in and out*

> *of all the rooms in God's house as though you were*
> *quite at home. You open the doors without knocking,*
> *and you hum on the stairs, and it isn't always hymns*
> *either. My aunt thinks you are not quite reverent;*
> *but, then, she can keep felt slippers on her mind*
> *without any trouble.*[1]

Yes, that is a quaint communication out of the old English past, and yet it is somehow descriptive of the somber point of view prevalent among many Christians today. But this "felt slippers on the mind" attitude doesn't match up with the exuberant joy and laughter that is God's gift to everyone who follows him and attempts to walk in Christ's footsteps.

Dr. Norman Vincent Peale in one of his sermons tells about the importance of joy and laughter as portrayed in a *Reader's Digest* article written by Bob Hope, the colorful and ageless radio and television personality. The setting for Bob Hope's story was 1948; General Dwight D. Eisenhower had just been appointed to the presidency of Columbia University. A great convocation of faculty and thousands of students came together to honor and greet the new president.

When General Eisenhower walked onto the platform, he confronted a super-serious audience that was at expectant attention in anticipation of a sedate call to serious study and sober living. However, the general displayed his world-famous grin and said, "Have fun! I mean it. The day that goes by without your having some fun—the day you don't enjoy life—is not only unnecessary but unchristian!"

General Eisenhower was, as usual, right on target. Over and over again the Bible spells out a clear message that God intends for us, his people, to be joyful and happy and, yes, to show it with hearty laughter. This doesn't mean, of course, that we will not experience difficult and trying times and endure both pain and sorrow. The ancient wisdom writer understood the ebb and flow of human emotions when he wrote that there would be "a time to weep" and "a time for mourning," but he counter-balanced that by saying that we would also have "a time to laugh" and "a time for dancing" (Eccles. 3:4 NEB).

Although the psalmist was well acquainted with the rigors and dangers of rustic life in the Judean hills and in the merciless climate and terrain of the Negev, he could still sing, "You will show me the way which leads to life: with You there is abundant joy; enjoyable things result continually from Your generosity."[2] And another wisdom writer quipped that when the people of God are happy "they smile" (Prov. 15:13 TEV).

Philo, the Alexandrian Jewish philosopher who lived in the time of Jesus, is quoted as saying, "God is the cre-ator of laughter that is good." But laughter and joy are not only God's creation, they are his gift to people in all of time, and as such, they, along with all of God's creation, are "very good." Martin Buber, the erudite Jewish theologian and philosopher commented on one occasion, "The heartbeat of life is holy joy."

The power and influence of joy and laughter are vividly illustrated in the lives of two extremely gifted and creative men. The first is Franz Joseph Haydn, whose genius sparked brightest in the mid-to-late 1700s and very early 1800s. He is credited with over one hundred symphonies and a vast array of other musical creations of varying styles. But Haydn's legacy also included a vigorous and intense devotion to God, as evidenced in part by his comment, "When I think of God, my heart is so full of joy that the notes leap and dance as they leave my pen; and since God has given me a cheerful heart, I serve him with a cheerful spirit." And out of this cheerful and joy-filled spirit came the magnificent oratorio *The Creation* and other compositions that have enriched the worship of Christians to this day.

The second gifted person who comes to mind is very much front and center on today's scene. Novelist James A. Michener was born into a Quaker household. He has this to say in his memoirs, "I was raised in an atmosphere of love, responsibility, and service, but what I remember most is the constant laughter in our home."[3] From *Tales of the South Pacific* in 1947 (a Pulitzer Prize winner) to *Mexico* in late 1992, James Michener's creative output of books has brought joy, happiness, and laughter to millions of people around the world—a glowing tribute to the constant laughter that dominated his Quaker boyhood home and has added spice and creative genius to all of his life and experiences.

This same spirit comes through clearly in a comment made by Dr. Samuel M. Shoemaker, that giant of a preacher who served major churches in New York and Pittsburgh a generation ago and whose writings have enriched the lives of thousands of people. For him, "The surest mark of a Christian is not faith, or even love, but joy." In truth, Sam Shoemaker had the faith, love, and devotion that contributed to the establishment of Alcoholics Anonymous and the Pittsburgh Experiment—both lifesaving institutions that have given new life and hope to thousands of hurting people. But it was his joyful and cheerful spirit that gave vigor to his ministry and attracted people to him. Indeed, it was his joy, faith, and love that doubtless prompted this comment by Dr. Billy Graham, "I doubt that any man in our generation has made a greater impact for God on the Christian world than did Samuel Shoemaker—a giant among men."[4]

Unfortunately, all too often skeptical people engaged in the struggle to find some kind of sense and order in our complex and complicated world are confronted by a somber and combative form of Christianity. Instead of infectious laughter bubbling up out of a full life enlivened by the Spirit of God, we Christians tend to sometimes model an exclusive and at times even an angry faith—one that erects towering barriers before anyone who does not see, understand, and express things our particular way.

Somehow, without intending to, our priorities have become confused. We have lost contact with the spirit of the angelic announcement to the awestruck and terrified Bethlehem shepherds, whose peaceful evening had been interrupted and disturbed by the intrusion of bright lights and angels in the night sky. According to the Gospel writer who described the scene, an angel in an effort to ease their terror said to them, "Do not be afraid; for see—I am bringing you good news of *great joy for all people*: to you is born this day in the city of David a Savior, who is the Messiah, the Lord" (Luke 2:10–11, italics mine). The coming of Jesus was a time for joy, laughter, and singing. His coming split history; the world and its people in all of time would never be the same again.

Somehow, too, we have become strangers to this Jesus of "good news and great joy" who with the passage of time became the Jesus who was attractive to the crowds and enjoyed a good time. Over and over again the Gospel writers picture Jesus being present at dinner parties and social functions. There are a number of references to Jesus attending dinner parties and intimate gatherings at the home of Mary, Martha, and Lazarus in Bethany. And we cannot help being a little amused over the grumblings of the self-righteous Pharisees because Jesus was at ease with tax collectors and sinners (Luke 15:1–2). He must have put them at ease by his caring and convivial spirit. While it is true that none of the Gospel writers speaks of Jesus' laughter, it is not stretching things to assume that people wanted to be around him because of his happy manner. After all, no one enjoys being around a grump, and harbingers of gloom aren't the least bit attractive and don't make good party and dinner company.

Jesus set the stage for this attitude toward all of life at the very earliest stages of his public ministry. The setting is what we know as the Sermon on the Mount. Matthew pictures Jesus speaking to vast crowds of people from a hillside, probably overlooking the Sea of Galilee. Dr. J. B. Phillips has given us a delightful translation of these beautiful words:

> How happy are the humble-minded. . . .
> How happy are those who know what sorrow
> means. . . .
> Happy are those who claim nothing. . . .
> Happy are those who are hungry and thirsty
> for goodness. . . .
> Happy are the merciful. . . .
> Happy are the utterly sincere. . . .
> Happy are those who make peace. . . .
> Happy are those who have suffered persecution
> for cause of goodness. . . .
> [Matt. 5:3–10 *Phillips*]

Perhaps we are more familiar with the King James Version and Revised Standard Version, which employ the word *blessed* where Dr. Phillips and other modern translators prefer the word *happy*. Jesus, of course, spoke in Aramaic, the common language of his day. We don't really have an English equivalent for the word Jesus used, but in effect he was saying, "Oh, how very blessed," or, "Oh, how effervescently happy." Pictured in the Beatitudes is a bubbling joyfulness and happiness of the kind usually expressed by exuberant laughter.

The late Dr. William Barclay, the erudite Scottish Bible scholar from Glasgow whose stated mission in life was to interpret biblical truth in the language of "the common man," says of these Beatitudes that they "are not the pious hopes of what shall be; they are not glowing, but nebulous prophecies of some future bliss; they are congratulations on what is. The blessedness which belongs to the Christian is not a blessedness which is postponed to some future world of glory; it is a blessedness which exists here and now. It is not something into which the Christian *will enter*; it is something into which he *has entered*."[5]

In other words, this gift from God is an unrestrained and glowing joy and happiness that floods through and over the life of the Christian in spite of the difficulties and heartaches that are inevitable in our human pilgrimage. These are not fanciful flashes of some future happiness but concrete assurances for the down-to-earth world in which we are now living.

Then toward the end of Jesus' ministry the Gospel writer moves us into some intimate scenes as he talks with his disciples and close friends. At one point he says, "I have said these things to you so that my joy may be in you, and that your joy may be complete" (John 15:11).

And between the Beatitudes and these last words of Jesus we have volumes of teachings and parables that give us glimpses into a very real and human Jesus whose humor seeps through and illuminates his profound teaching. Jesus, in fact, was a master storyteller whose comparisons and descriptions were often flavored with the subtlest forms of humor—irony and exaggeration. The Gospel writers of Matthew, Mark, and Luke especially seemed to catch the earthy humor in Jesus' teachings. And while laughter is not spoken of, many of the scenes and settings give strong hints of a smile and even laughter.

Over the years I've been enriched and challenged in reading those New Testament books credited to the apostle Paul. I've always had the notion that he was a very intense and no-nonsense kind of a person, not much given to seeing or expressing the lighter and more humorous and happy side of things. Yet I have to believe there was a happy and joyous side to this great apostle— possibly even to the point of laughter now and then. In writing to his close Christian friends in the Roman colony of Philippi, he gave them and us a hint of his feelings when he wrote, "I want you to be happy, always happy in the Lord; I repeat, what I want is your happiness" (Phil. 4:4 JB).

As we reflect on the Bible drama and on the vast array of Christian saints who have moved back and forth on the stage of history, we are no doubt easily convinced that God has indeed given to us and to his people in all of time his gift of joy, laughter, and happiness. It was said of the early Christians that they could be easily identified because of their joyful and loving manner. We have to believe that they did not go around with long faces and worried creases in their foreheads. Rather, they had accepted God's gift of joy and laughter and had nurtured that gift until it could be readily seen in every part of their lives.

God has given us so much, and the challenge for each of us as believers in Jesus Christ is to respond with contagious joy. Author Harold Kushner very wisely put his finger on an extremely important point when he wrote, "In the Talmud, the collective wisdom of the rabbis of the first five centuries, it is written, 'In the world to come, each of us will be called to account for all the good things God put on earth which we refused to enjoy.'"[6]

The inspired writers of our Bible insisted that the world and all of God's magnificent creation is ours to enjoy. And for the Christian it is a big and wonderful world as described so often by the writers of the Psalms—a world in which the fingerprints of God are seen in all that he has made.

One of the most winsome and electric television per-sonalities of the past generations was Archbishop Fulton J. Sheen. He beautifully captured the idea that the Christ-ian way of life was intended to be one of unrestrained joy and laughter. His quick wit and penchant for humorous and delightful stories coupled with a winsome and conta-gious smile made him one of the most convincing voices for God that has ever shown up on television. In his auto-biography Bishop Sheen made this sagacious comment, "The amount of humor that anyone gets out of the world is the size of the world in which he lives."[7]

Any expression of Christianity that fails to illuminate God's gift of joy and laughter is incomplete and inade-quate. While the joy-filled Christian is aware of all of the hurt, suffering, and injustice present in our world, he or she is unquestionably convinced that God is still in charge—ultimately, all's right in God's world!

4

Say Yes to
GOD'S GIFT OF PRAYER

*The paradox of prayer is that we have to learn
how to pray while we can only receive it as a gift.*

Henri J. M. Nouwen

*Our Father, who has set a restlessness in our hearts
and made us all seekers after that which we can
never fully find. . . keep us at tasks too hard for us,
that we may be driven to Thee for strength.*

A prayer Eleanor Roosevelt carried in her purse

*T*he year was 1952. The setting was Rice University
stadium in Houston, Texas. The event was the citywide
Billy Graham Crusade. The audience was made up of
forty-five thousand attentive and eager listeners.

I was sitting on the platform with tears in my eyes.
Roy was at the podium, speaking. It was Roy's first witness to a crowd of this size.

"Dale worked with God to bring me something I had longed for all of my life—peace. Materially speaking, for years I had nothing. Then for years I had much. But I soon learned that having too much is worse than having too little. Nothing ever seemed quite right. I was restless, confused, unsatisfied. But then I learned that the power of prayer and the feeling of spiritual blessedness and the love of Jesus have no price tags."

The stadium was locked in a dead silence. It seemed that all of the forty-five thousand people were holding their breath for what would come next. Roy went on to describe the strength he gained through daily prayer and reflective Bible reading. Then he closed his witness by denying the published rumors that he was thinking of leaving show business and becoming an evangelist. "If I was going to be an evangelist," he smiled, "I guess I'd have to do it on horseback, because being a cowboy is all I know." And as Roy's smile gave way to a wide boyish grin, the crowd melted and broke out with thunderous applause.

Yes, God's gift of prayer has been a powerful sustaining force in our home for many years—through difficult times as well as in good times. And this we know for sure, prayer—agonizing prayer—saw both of us through the two years that we cared for our little Robin, our Down's syndrome baby, our *Angel Unawares*. When she left us to be with her heavenly Father, it was prayer that kept us steady. It was prayer—ours and those of our friends—

that saw us through the tragic deaths of our daughter Debbie on the church bus and our son Sandy in Germany.

More recently, Roy and I have had reason to rely with deep feelings of gratitude on the gift of prayer as each of us has weathered heart attacks and surgery—mine as recently as the spring of 1992. In all of this we've been reminded over and over again of the definition of prayer given us by one of our Bible teachers. She told us that prayer should be: first, praise of God; second, thanksgiving for his love and guidance; and, third, petition for ourselves and our needs. And the final word was, "You can trust him implicitly for the answer."

How true! Yet there have been those days—yes, weeks and even months—when it seemed that God was strangely silent to my heartaches and hurts. But slowly I've come to understand just a little bit the truth behind these thoughts of Henry Ward Beecher, the powerful nineteenth-century preacher, who wrote in his little book entitled *Aids to Prayer,* "Think not that God's silence is coldness or indifference! When Christ stood by the dead, the silence of tears interpreted his sympathy more wonderfully than even that voice which afterwards called back the footsteps of the brother [Lazarus], and planted them in life again. When birds are on the nest, preparing to bring forth life, they never sing."

An unidentified writer made this intriguing comment, "There is no music in a rest, but there is the making of music in it." In the melody of our lives' experiences we often come to those times of silence and "rests." It is important in such moments not to feel that the life-melody is over but to look expectantly for the next movement to begin. God is still the divine Conductor.

In our humanness we fall victim so often to the notion that God should act on our schedule and timetable and in ways that we can readily understand. There is an ever-present danger that we may come to see prayer as a form of heavenly room service. We tend to lose sight of the truth that the purpose of prayer is not to change God or to activate him. Rather the purpose of prayer is to change us. I like the way author Søren Kierkegaard expressed this idea, "Prayer does not change God, but changes him who prays."

Author Henri Nouwen enriches our understanding of prayer as he writes that when "prayer makes us reach out to God, not on our own but on his terms, then prayer pulls us away from self-preoccupations, encourages us to leave familiar ground, and challenges us to enter into a new world which cannot be contained within the narrow boundaries of our mind and heart." Then Dr. Nouwen adds, "Prayer, therefore, is a great adventure because the God with whom we enter into a new relationship is greater than we are and defies all calculations and predictions."[1]

Along this same line of thought is a comment credited to the late William Temple, the ninety-eighth Archbishop of Canterbury, "When I say my prayers, I find that coincidences begin to happen." On the other hand, it is important that we strive for an understanding of prayer that avoids it misuse. Dr. James Houston cautions against this in his perceptive book entitled *The Transforming Friendship*, "It is alarmingly easy for prayer to become a kind of magical device which we use to get our own way."[2]

This leads us in our Christian pilgrimage to not only say *Yes* to God's gift of prayer but to also pose the same request that Jesus' disciples put to him one day. Luke speaks of the incident in these words, "Once, in a certain place, Jesus was at prayer. When he ceased, one of his disciples said, 'Lord, teach us to pray' " (Luke 11:1 NEB).

Jesus' response to this request was simple and uncomplicated but very much to the point:

> *Father, may your name be honoured—may your kingdom come! Give us each day the bread we need, and forgive us our sins, for we forgive anyone who owes anything to us; and keep us clear of temptation.*
>
> [Luke 11:2–4 *Phillips*]

This has become known as "the Lord's Prayer"—certainly the supreme model for us of the gift of prayer. While the Luke wording of Jesus' response to his disciples is considerably shorter than the one found in the Gospel of Matthew (see Matt. 6:9–13), it gives us in a nutshell everything essential to our coming to an understanding of how we are to use God's gift of prayer and what we are to pray for.

Space prohibits me from making an exhaustive commentary on the Lord's Prayer, but in a few words I want to express a little of what it has come to mean to me. First, Jesus prays, "Father." This was the traditional opening for any Jewish prayer. However, in this instance Jesus used a most untraditional Aramaic word for *Father*—*Abba*. This is the word a child would have used in speaking to a human father. *Father* as Jesus used it here gives us a sense of intimacy, respect, and reverence that shifts prayer from a ritual to a profound personal and intimate experience and relationship—quite the opposite to a flippant or casual approach.

For Jesus, the Father was not a vague, faraway entity but an intimate and nearby Father—one who cares deeply about everything that concerns us. The apostle Paul expressed it this way for those first-century Christians who were struggling with the idea of this kind of God:

> To prove that you are sons, God has sent into our
> hearts the Spirit of his Son, crying "Abba! Father!"
> You are therefore no longer a slave but a son, and
> if a son, then also by God's own act an heir.

[Gal. 4:6 NEB]

Next in the model prayer Jesus said, "May your name be honoured" or "hallowed be your name." This heavenly Father of ours is also the Creator-God who spoke the universe into existence and is to be revered. In the words of Isaiah the prophet, he is the Holy One. Over the centuries Christian believers have struggled long and hard for a human understanding of God, and in that struggle the temptation to bring him down to our size often rears its ugly head.

Human experience makes it clear that we will never understand God in this life, but we are to revere all that we do understand him to be. Saint Augustine put it very succinctly when he said, "If you have understood, then what you have understood is not God."

We get a deeper understanding of what is happening in this prayer Jesus taught his disciples as we realize that the reference to God's Name goes far beyond the way we use the word. To the Jews *name* referred to a person's total character. To pray, "may your name be honoured," means "far more than knowing that God's name is Jehovah. It means that those who know the whole character and mind and heart of God will gladly put their trust in him."[3] And in praying "May your kingdom come," we are asking that God's will may become a reality to Christian believers now and in all of the future.

The writer of the Matthew version of the prayer adds this sentence, "Thy will be done in earth, as it is in heaven"

(Matt. 6:10 KJV). It seems to me that this is the central petition of the Lord's Prayer even as it is to be central in all of our praying. Only then can we move on to the remaining petitions of the prayer.

A close look at how prayer is treated in the Book of Acts gives us the pattern the early Christians followed under the leadership and teaching of the apostles—their prayers were always for God's will to be done, even as they prayed for others. For them, and for us, prayer is intended to be an intimate part of all of life—not something reserved to be used when we're in trouble or at eleven o'clock on Sunday morning.

As I mentioned earlier, Dr. Samuel Shoemaker in his books and sermons had a most perceptive way of conveying truth. On one occasion he said, "Prayer is not calling in the fire department; prayer is seeking to live so that the house does not get on fire. Prayer is not the 'last resort,' it is the first thought in every situation…Prayer is communion between two 'people' who increasingly know each other. And one of these 'people' is very decidedly a Senior Partner in the relationship."[4]

So far, in the Lord's Prayer our attention has been focused on God:

Our Father in heaven,
hallowed be your name.
Your kingdom come.

Your will be done,
on earth as it is in heaven.

[Matt. 6:9–10]

Now the focus shifts to us and our needs:

Give us this day our daily bread.
And forgive us our debts,
as we also have forgiven our debtors.
And do not bring us to the time of trial,
but rescue us from the evil one.

[Matt. 6:11–13]

First, Jesus directed our thoughts to God and his will for everyone. Now comes the acknowledgment that this same God is concerned about and equal to our needs here and now; he forgives our sins and wipes out our debts; and, finally, we can look to the future in confidence, knowing that the Father will support us in our times of testing and trial.

Behind all of Jesus' teaching is the truth that the Father is a God of love who cares intimately for each one of us. St. Teresa of Avila, a devout sixteenth-century Spanish Christian, captured the true meaning of prayer when she said, "Prayer is not a matter of thinking a great deal but of loving a great deal." In writing to Christians everywhere and in all of time, the writer of the Book of Jude counseled his readers with these words, "But you, my friends, must fortify yourselves in your most sacred faith. Continue to pray in the power of the Holy Spirit. *Keep yourselves in the love of God*" (Jude 1:20–21 NEB, italics mine).

Reflecting on God's gift of prayer to people like us is an awesome experience. In a sermon entitled "The World's Greatest Power: PRAYER" Dr. Norman Vincent Peale asked the question, "What is the greatest power in the universe?" In response he adds, "Is it the enormous force of the hurricane or the tornado, or the tidal wave, or the earthquake, or the exploding volcano?" He then defines this power in these electric phrases, "I believe that it is the mechanism by which man on earth establishes a connection that provides the flow of power between the mighty Creator and himself, between the great God who scattered the stars in the infinite night sky and the crea-ture made in his own image: man. The flow of power between the Creator and man is the world's greatest power. And it is released and transmitted by means of a mechanism known as prayer."[5] But it is a power that calls for action on our part if it is to be effective.

One of the greatest and most endearing preachers of the past generation was Dr. Paul S. Rees. He had the knack of packing profound truth into a few words, "If we are willing to take hours on end to learn to play the piano, or operate a computer, or fly an airplane, it is sheer nonsense for us to imagine that we can learn the high art of getting guidance through communion with the Lord without being willing to set aside time for it. It is no accident that the Bible speaks of prayer as a form of waiting on God."[6]

In the midst of our busy and hectic lives a first step to this "waiting on God" may involve putting into practice an idea suggested by Dr. Frank Laubach. Picking up on the pray-without-ceasing principle as expressed by the apostle Paul, Dr. Frank suggests instant or quick prayers right in the middle of the hustle and bustle of life: A sentence prayer while sitting in the doctor's waiting room, "Lord, bless the doctor and give him wisdom." Or a prayer for Jane after dialing her number and waiting for an answer, "Bless Jane, Lord, as she takes on her responsibilities in her new job." Or while waiting for a bus or a taxi or an airplane, "Oh God, guide the hand of the driver (pilot) and give us a safe trip." Or while sitting prayerfully in your pew at church waiting for the service to begin, "Father, speak to me this morning and help me to be open to you and everyone around me." Waiting at the signal for the red light to turn green…while standing in the grocery checkout line…while walking four laps in the mall or while walking the dog in the early morning hours—all of these daily routines offer the opportunity for prayer fragments that can enrich our own lives and the lives of the people we are praying for.

In the early centuries of the Christian church the Desert Fathers, quite likely in the vicinity of Mount Sinai, put together a very simple ten-word prayer that has become known as "the Jesus Prayer": "Lord Jesus Christ, Son of God, have mercy on me." Throughout the centuries both clergy and lay people have seen in these few words the summation of the Christian faith, and it is used widely by people who pray in all parts of the world as a means of grace and a sustainer of the faith.

An unknown writer left us this gem:

> *Prayer is so simple;*
> *It is like quietly opening a door and slipping into the*
>   *very presence of God.*
> *There in the stillness*
> *To listen to his voice, perhaps to petition*
>   *Or only to listen.*
> *It matters not,*
>   *Just to be there, in his presence...*
> *Is prayer.*

Another unknown writer left behind these incisive reflections on the Lord's Prayer.

> *I cannot pray **our**,*
>   *if my faith has no room for others and their needs.*
> *I cannot pray **Father**,*
>   *if I do not demonstrate this relationship to God*
>   *in my daily living.*

I cannot pray **who art in heaven**,
> if all my interests and pursuits are in earthly things.

I cannot pray **hallowed be Thy name**,
> if I'm not striving with God's help to be holy.

I cannot pray **Thy kingdom come**,
> if I am unwilling or resentful of having it in my life.

I cannot pray **on earth as it is in heaven**,
> unless I am truly ready to give myself to God's
> service here and now.

I cannot pray **give us this day our daily bread**,
> without expending honest effort for it,
> or if I would withhold from my neighbor the bread
> that I receive.

I cannot pray **forgive us our trespasses as we forgive
those who trespass against us**,
> if I continue to harbor a grudge against anyone.

I cannot pray **lead us not into temptation**,
> if I deliberately choose to remain in a situation
> where I am likely to be tempted.

I cannot pray **deliver us from evil**,
> if I am not prepared to fight and resist evil.

I cannot pray **Thine is the kingdom**,
> if I am unwilling to obey the king.

I cannot pray **Thine is the power and the glory**,
> if I'm seeking power for myself and my own glory first.

I cannot pray **forever and ever**,
> if I am too anxious about each day's affairs.

*I cannot pray **Amen**,*
unless I can honestly say,
"Cost what it may, this is my prayer."

Our pastor, the Rev. William Hanson, prayed this prayer, which I have taken as my own, "Lord, we confess that we cling to a safe and comfortable faith. We are not looking for challenges, and we do not like to take risks. Forgive us for taming your gospel and reshaping your teachings to our liking. Forgive us, Lord, and help us to break free from the false security of our own comfort to the true security of faith. Change us in such a way that we may become willing to risk our hearts and lives in following and serving you. Amen."

Say Yes to
GOD'S GIFT OF WONDER

If you accept this Gospel
and become Christ's man,
you will stumble upon wonder upon wonder,
and every wonder true.

Brendan to King Brude

*T*he ancient Judean poet-sheepherder was divinely inspired one night to write and reflect on his overwhelming awareness of all that was going on around him. These were his thoughts, and we can be eternally grateful that his words have been preserved for us.

Oh God, how full of wonder and splendor you are!
I see the reflections of your beauty and hear
the sounds of your majesty wherever I turn.
Even the babbling of babes and the laughter of
children spell out your name in
indefinable syllables.

When I gaze into star-studded skies and attempt
to comprehend the vast distances,
I contemplate in utter amazement my
Creator's concern for me.
I am dumbfounded that you should care personally
about me.
And yet You have made me in Your image.
You have called me Your son.
You have ordained me as Your priest and chosen
me to be Your servant.
You have assigned to me the fantastic responsibility
of carrying on Your
creative activity.
O God, how full of wonder and splendor
You are![1]

In this present-day translation of the awe-inspiring psalm we catch the poet's almost inexpressible amazement at the wonder of God's world. At the same time, there is the awareness that in some mysterious way in creating us in his image he has bequeathed to us the gift of wonder. We sense his utter amazement over everything that comes from God.

Like the psalmist on a star-studded night, Robert Louis Stevenson, the gifted nineteenth-century novelist and essayist, captured this sense of wonder one night in Calistoga at the north end of California's Napa Valley. His magnificently descriptive prose reveals the depth of his feelings.

> *I have never seen such a night... The sky itself was*
> *of a ruddy, powerful, nameless, changing color,*
> *dark and glossy like a serpent's back. The stars by*
> *innumerable millions stuck boldly forth like lamps.*
> *The Milky Way was bright like a moonlit cloud; half*
> *heaven seemed Milky Way. The greater luminaries*
> *each more clearly than a winter's moon. Their light*
> *was dyed in every sort of color—red, like fire; blue,*
> *like steel; green, like the tracks of sunset; and so*
> *sharply did each stand forth in its own lustre that*
> *there was no appearance of that flat, star-spangled*
> *arch we know so well in pictures, but all the hollow*
> *of heaven was one chaos of contesting luminaries—*
> *a hurly-burly of stars.*

While Robert Louis Stevenson made no direct reference in this descriptive piece to God as the author of the wonders he was seeing, we know that in some way he was in tune with the Creator of it all, for in another piece he said, "There is nothing but God's grace. We walk upon it; we breathe it; we live and die by it; it makes the nails and axles of the Universe."

People throughout all of human history—from the beginning, whenever that was, to the present—have in their thoughtful moments been moved in reverence by the wonders of God's world. In contemplating those wonders, many have seen them as testimonies of His fatherly and caring involvement in everything that concerns us.

Yes, there are those who have been unwilling to acknowledge God in the wonders of our universe and others who claim to believe that all of this, including life itself, is the result of some kind of cosmic accident. Such ideas, though, just do not square with our deepest feelings. It has been suggested that the chance of life originating from some sort of cosmic accident would be comparable to a leather-bound copy of an unabridged dictionary appearing full-blown after an explosion in a book manufacturing plant.

Far more believable and satisfying is this assertion of the psalmist,

> By the word of the LORD the heavens were made,
> and all their host by the breath of his mouth.
> He gathered the waters of the sea as in a bottle;
> He put the deeps in storehouses.
> Let all the earth fear the LORD;
> let all the inhabitants of the world stand in awe
> of him.
> For he spoke, and it came to be;
> he commanded and it stood firm.

[Ps. 33:6–9]

In a moment of inspiration the ancient wisdom writer agreed with the psalmist when he wrote,

> *The LORD created the earth by his wisdom;*
> *by his knowledge he set the sky in place.*
> *His wisdom caused the rivers to flow*
> *and the clouds to give rain to the earth.*

[Prov. 3:19–20 TEV]

But perhaps the most amazing of God's wonders is his gift of wonder to us, as we saw earlier when, in a flash of insight, the psalmist reminded us that we are made in God's image and are his chosen sons and daughters. Having said that, the psalmist added, "You have assigned to me [us] the fantastic responsibility of carrying on Your creative activity."[2]

What an incredible wonder and assignment! What a glorious legacy we have as God's special people. It is hard to believe, and yet as we view the wonders of just the last few years, we can only say, "Thank you, Lord, for the gift of wonder." For in our lifetime we have come to take the airplane for granted, while a generation ago people would dash out of their houses and search the skies at the sound of an engine overhead. The average speed of the Mayflower when it crossed the Atlantic with our Puritan ancestors was two miles per hour. It took weeks then to cover the distance, and now our modern airplanes make it over the same route in four to six hours.

Not long ago we were glued to our television sets—another wonder that God made possible—as we watched the first Mercury spacecraft make its foray into the heavens. Next followed several Apollo flights. In just a few short years God-given genius and creative know-how have taken astronauts to the moon, and robot space vehicles have been launched and are probing deepest space.

God-given image-of-God wonder was described in considerable detail in a September 1990 article by Professor Carl Sagan of Cornell University as he wrote about Voyager 1, launched in 1981 and speeding through space at an incredible speed. Professor Sagan wrote that in February of 1990 while "the ship was speeding away from the fading sun at 40,000 miles an hour" it was overtaken by "an unusual and unexpected set of instructions." In response to those instructions "it turned its cameras toward the now-distant planets. Pointing from one spot in the sky to another, it took sixty pictures and stored them in its tape recorder. Then, slowly, in March, April, and May it radioed the images back to earth."

According to Professor Sagan, "The spacecraft was 3.7 billion miles away from earth, so far away that it took each pixel (individual picture elements) five and one-half hours, traveling at the speed of light, to reach us." The picture of earth that accompanied this article was a pale blue dot about the size of a pencil point.

Referring to the picture of the pale blue dot, Professor

Sagan continued, "Look at earth in this picture.... That's here. That's home. That's us. And on that dot everyone you love, everyone you know, everyone you ever heard of, every human being who ever was, lived out their lives. Every act of human heroism or betrayal, the sum total of human joy and suffering...every king and peasant, mother and father, hopeful child, inventor and explorer, moral teacher and corrupt politician, every saint and sinner in the history of our species lived here."[3]

Time and human ingenuity and God's revelation in our Bible have not afforded us a hint as to whether there is life in any part of God's universe except on that pale blue dot. But this we know for sure—God has populated our earth with people made in his image. People who "see the reflections" of his beauty "and hear the sounds" of his majesty as expressed by the psalmist. And what is most astounding are the psalm writer's words, "You [God] have assigned to me [us] the fantastic responsibility of carrying on Your [God's] creative activity."[4]

Next comes the knotty question: How can we possibly, under any stretch of imagination, carry on God's creative activities? The answer is obvious: We can't—not in our own strength and ability. But as a result of all that occurred in life, death, and resurrection of Jesus Christ and our commitment to him—we *can*!

As wonder-filled as the technology of the nineteenth and twentieth centuries is, including our amazing space exploits, God's greatest wonder occurred some two thousand years ago when the resurrection of Jesus Christ from the Garden tomb on that first Easter morning revolutionized all of creation. Indeed, this is the wonder that exceeds all others. This staggering event split history—nothing would ever be the same again!

The immediate impact of that Easter wonder was viewed in living color through the dramatic change in the lives and actions of Jesus' core followers. Just a day or two before the resurrection event and following the crucifixion, the disciples had gone into hiding in terror. Now those once fear-paralyzed people moved out into the open with seeming reckless abandon in their Spirit intoxication. Where earlier they had quivered in fear, now they were bold in their ardent concern for the physical, social, and spiritual needs of people. The same Peter who just a few weeks before had insisted he didn't even know Jesus stood boldly before the Jerusalem crowd and announced that Jesus whom they crucified had risen from the dead and had returned to his Father—this Jesus was "both Lord and Messiah" (Acts 2:14–36).

Further proof of the revolutionary change in the attitudes and lives of the disciples is given to us by Luke in his Book of Acts drama as he writes about Peter and John who were accosted by a beggar at the gate of the temple. They didn't respond to his request for money with a sermon or a proof text. Instead Peter looked deep into the beggar's expectant eyes, stated bluntly that he didn't have any money, but then reached out, took the man by the hand, and said, "In the name of Jesus Christ of Nazareth, *walk!*" With that, the man not only got to his feet and stood, but "he walked about, leaping and thanking God" (Acts 3:1–8 *Phillips*). I repeat, this is the same Peter who not long before had cursed and denied he knew Jesus at all.

To emphasize even more for his readers the dramatic change that had occurred, Luke wrote,

> *Many signs and wonders were now happening among the people.... People would bring out their sick into the streets and lay them down on stretchers or beds, so that as Peter came by at least his shadow might fall upon some of them.... And they were all cured.*

[Acts 5:15–16 *Phillips*]

The late Leslie Weatherhead, who for many years was the pastor of London's City Temple, in his remarkable book entitled *Key Next Door* gave us this wonder-filled summation of the atmosphere of those early days: "Within seven weeks they—the hunted frightened fugitives—had become flaming missionaries and willing martyrs ready to lay down their lives rather than deny the truth of His risen glory and His transforming power. Christianity was launched on its world mission."[5]

It was this kind of devotion and courage that launched the dramatic missionary movement of the eighteenth and nineteenth centuries that took the gospel to India, China, and Japan under the direction of such missionary leaders as Adoniram Judson and Hudson Taylor. And that early launching of the modern missionary movement was carried into the twentieth century by Dr. E. Stanley Jones, Charles and Lettie Cowman, Dr. A. B. Simpson, Dr. Frank Laubach, and a vast army of courageous people who witnessed to the power of the gospel in the South Seas, Latin America, and around the world.

Wonder of wonders, the stage was set for all of this by the attitude and actions of those first-century Christians. They had no time for bickering or criticism of one another. There was no jockeying for position, for front row seats, or for honor. Instead Luke described them in these words,

> Among the large number who had become believers
> **there was complete agreement of heart and soul.**
> Not one of them claimed any of his possessions
> as his own but everything was common property.
> The apostles continued to give their witness to the
> resurrection of the Lord Jesus with great force, and
> a wonderful spirit of generosity pervaded the whole
> fellowship.
>
> [Acts 4:32–33 *Phillips*, emphasis mine]

The drama and wonder of the resurrection miracle from those early days of Christianity until today is beautifully expressed by author Frederick Buechner. In *Telling the Truth* he says it is "the outlandishness of God who does impossible things with impossible people."[6]

It is easy for us to identify with the "impossible people." But how grateful we are for the "outlandishness" of God, who through Jesus Christ has given us the fantastic experience of carrying on his creative activity.

Wonder of wonders!

6

Say Yes to
GOD'S GIFT OF FRIENDSHIP

*The friend who can be silent with us
in a moment of despair or confusion,
who can stay with us
in an hour of grief and bereavement,
who can tolerate not-knowing, not-curing,
not-healing, and face with us
the reality of our powerlessness,
that is the friend who cares.*

Bernie S. Segal

*B*eing a friend and having friends are, without question, among the greatest gifts of God's magnificent creation schemes—awesome gifts to each of us from a caring heavenly Father.

It is easy, though, in the frantic rush of our busy twenty-four-hour days to become so self-preoccupied that we fail to be a friend. Yet as we progress through the various stages of our lives, we are conscious in our more thoughtful and honest moments of just how much we need each other for the enrichment of our own life experiences and personal growth.

In the early 1940s, through an intriguing combination of circumstances, a Hollywood agent named Art Rush became a part of my life. Following a stint as a singer on CBS radio station WBBM in Chicago, I had signed a one-year contract with Twentieth Century Fox motion picture studios in Hollywood under the guidance of an agent named Joe Rivken. During that year I got just two bit parts, and all the signs seemed to indicate that my contract would not be renewed. The studio moguls had decided that I looked too much like their current top star, Betty Grable, to be built up and featured.

At that same time I confess that I felt like a fish out of water—I understood radio, but motion pictures were something else. So, I asked Joe Rivken to recommend a Hollywood agent who was at home in the radio world. I remember Joe's response as if it were yesterday, "There is just one man in all of Hollywood that I would trust you with. And his name is Art Rush."

I contacted Art Rush immediately, and arrangements were made for me to sing for him and his wife, Mary Jo. Following the audition, which went off well, Art said, "I think I know just the spot for you. There's an opening for a female vocalist on the 'Chase and Sanborn Hour' "—the show that featured Edgar Bergen and Charlie McCarthy, Don Ameche, and orchestra leader Ray Noble.

Art arranged for the audition, and I sang for Edgar Bergen, Ray Noble, and the show's producer Tony Sanford. I felt pretty sure I had the job when that crazy puppet Charlie McCarthy gave me a shrill whistle through his wooden mouth. I smiled, Edgar Bergen smiled, and Art Rush smiled. A few days later I signed a contract, and for the next thirty-nine weeks I appeared on the show as the featured female vocalist. It was a choice spot—prime time, five o'clock Sunday afternoon. This was just the break I needed on one of the most popular shows of that time.

During those weeks Art Rush and I were together a great deal. In our conversations I learned that Art was a devout Christian. As a young man he had gone to Bethany College with the idea of becoming a minister, but he soon felt this was not his calling. However, Art's commitment to God remained the most important thing in his life. He said to me one time, "Dale, God is the Director of my life." This wasn't hard to believe, because his actions and soft-spoken demeanor squared with his words.

Again and again in our conversations Art brought up the name of a singing cowboy client of his, Roy Rogers. Art was very proud of Roy, who at that time was number one in western pictures. We had not met yet, but a little later I was singing at Edwards Air Force Base in California's Mojave Desert and was scheduled to appear with Roy Rogers and the Sons of the Pioneers. It was then Art introduced me to his singing cowboy protégé. No sky rockets went off, and no bells rang in my head. Roy Rogers seemed to me at that time to be just a shy, mannerly cowboy with striking good looks and a nice singing voice—nothing more, nothing less.

In the meantime I'd had a call from a person at Republic Studios who had heard me sing, and I was asked to go out there and audition for them. That audition produced a one-year contract, and two weeks later I was in rehearsal for a movie entitled, "Swing Your Partner." During that year I did seven more films and must have toured every army base in the southwestern United States.

After my Republic contract was renewed, Mr. Yates, the head of Republic Studios, called me one day and said, "Our Roy Rogers westerns have been doing very well, and I think they would go over even better if we had a female lead who was a singer and had a radio following. I think you are what we are looking for." Then he added, "Rehearsals for 'The Cowboy and the Senorita' will begin next week. You're the senorita." The year was 1944.

B-Westerns weren't exactly what I had in mind for a career, but I went along with Mr. Yates's directive, and before that year was over I had made three more pictures with Roy. Finally, after a series of events, I left the studio and went my own way. In 1947, however, while I was doing an engagement in Atlantic City, I looked out into the audience and saw Art Rush and Roy Rogers. We talked after the show, and it wasn't long before I was back at Republic working with Roy.

On New Year's Eve of 1947 Roy and I were married at the Flying-L Ranch near Davis, Oklahoma, with Art Rush as Roy's best man and Mary Jo Rush as my matron of honor. For the next fifty-some years Art Rush represented both Roy and me. He was the closest and best friend either of us ever had. He was with us in our successes, and he shared those agonizing moments at the deaths of our three children.

Roy and I have many poignant memories of time spent with Art, but etched into our minds forever is a picture of him the night before he died. He couldn't speak, but Art looked at us as we stood at the foot of his bed, and with a light in his eyes he formed these words with his lips, "I love you."

Art Rush truly epitomized the "true friend" described by one of the Bible's wisdom writers,

> *Some friends play at friendship*
> *but a true friend sticks closer*
> *than one's nearest kin.*
>
> [Prov.18:24]

In another place this same writer said, "A friend loves at all times" (Prov. 17:17). The very wise and insightful writer of the apocryphal Book of Ecclesiasticus further described what Art Rush means to us,

A faithful friend is a secure shelter;
whoever finds one has found a treasure.
A faithful friend is beyond price;
his worth is more than money can buy.
A faithful friend is an elixir of life,
found only by those who fear the Lord.
The man [person] who fears the Lord keeps his
  friendships in repair,
for he treats his neighbour as himself.

[Ecclus. 6:14–17 NEB]

Keeping our friendships in repair is a salient ingredient of our relationships. It has been said that we have a custodial responsibility to maintain our friendships.

Noted Christian historian and author Dr. Martin E. Marty has written a marvelous book on friendship. In it he speaks of friendship as being "a gift of God." He writes, "To be a friend may mean to be the most important person in the world to someone else over a period of years."[1] Most certainly, friendship involves giving ourselves unreservedly to others; it involves accepting others unconditionally and being *with* them—really being with them in their failures as well as in their triumphs.

As I have continued to reflect on the enormous impact Art Rush had on our lives through his gift of friendship, I have been reminded of a quality of his that I think made him the kind of a person he was. He *really* listened to us—

he didn't just *hear* us, he *listened* to us. I've come to understand that we hear with our ears, but we listen with our
hearts! Art always listened to us with his heart.

The Bible's wisdom writers have a great deal to say,
overtly and covertly, about the importance of listening in
our relationships. This idea has its greatest expression in
the Bible story of King Solomon, who achieved greatness
because of his wisdom. When Solomon was crowned king
upon the death of his Father David, we're told that God
appeared to him in a dream or vision and asked him,
"What shall I give you?" Solomon responded with a
lengthy answer, but the heart of what he asked for was
simply this, "Give thy servant…a heart with skill to listen,
so that he may govern thy people justly and distinguish
good from evil" (1 Kings 3:9 NEB). The New Revised
Standard Version of this same verse reads, "Give your servant therefore an understanding mind." Both readings are
quite correct with the original Hebrew—*listening* and an
understanding mind are one and the same.

The ancient wise men of Israel well understood the
importance of listening, and time hasn't changed that. We
all have a desperate need to listen to our friends and to be
listened to.

Paul Tillich, noted theologian of a past generation
wrote somewhere, "The first duty of love is to listen."
Another very wise person is reported to have said, "Listening is a key to *knowing* and *understanding*." It seems to me

that is what friendship is all about—it is knowing and understanding another person and being known and understood by another person.

Throughout the Bible we encounter a parade of friendships that serve as models for us. Perhaps the classic and most profoundly moving story is found in the Old Testament book of First Samuel. In chapters 18, 19, and 20 the writer features the relationship between Jonathan, King Saul's son, and David, the shepherd-boy giant-killer from Bethlehem. The biblical writer tells us that "Saul's son Jonathan was deeply attracted to David and came to love him as much as he loved himself. Jonathan swore eternal friendship with David because of his deep affection for him" (1 Sam. 18:1, 3 TEV). As proof that this was not just a surface friendship, Prince Jonathan sealed the relationship publicly, at considerable risk to himself, by giving David his royal robe and his prized weapons—his sword, bow, and belt—all emblems of his royal position as the king's son and a prince in Israel.

Two things leap out at me in this Jonathan and David friendship story. First, the ancient and very wise writer makes the point that Jonathan loved David "as his own soul" (NRSV)—as he loved himself. With Jonathan, as with each of us, the capacity for friendship emerged from healthy self-esteem and self-acceptance. This idea was first suggested by the Leviticus writer centuries before when he recorded God's words to Moses, "You shall love your neighbor as *yourself*" (Lev. 19:18, italics mine). Jonathan seemed to understand that well and applied it to his own life.

The second thing that stands out sharply is that David accepted Jonathan's gift of friendship and the symbols of that gift. From that time on, in spite of setbacks and reverses, David moved steadily toward becoming Israel's greatest king and earned a place in God's Hall of Fame as listed in Hebrews 11. I have to believe that his early friendship with Jonathan was a vital chapter in David's story.

Dr. Leslie Weatherhead wrote in one of his books, "If I were to say in one sentence what Christianity is, I think I should say that it was the acceptance of Christ's friendship." Then he added, "Christianity began in friendship."[2]

How true! Early in the story of Jesus we understand how important friends and friendship are to him, and from him we learn an invaluable lesson. We see in Jesus' actions and selections that he was inclusive. By contrast, in exercising our own gift of friendship, we are prone more often than not to select for friends only those people who see, believe, and express things the way we do. Most of the time our friends are *our* kind of people who are comfortable with our particular patterns and prejudices. All too often we insist that *our* friends think and speak only with our social and spiritual vocabulary.

When Jesus selected the twelve men to be his special friends and followers at the very beginning of his public life, he was amazingly inclusive. They were ordinary, everyday people—most of them were rugged and weather-beaten fishermen. Early on we learn that James and John were hot-tempered, self-serving, and instinctively ambitious. Peter was volatile and impetuous, and more often than not suffered from foot-in-mouth disease. Matthew was a customs and tax collector—a profession notorious for greed and crooked dealing, despised by the Jews and classed with murderers and robbers. In fact, tax collectors were excluded from the judicial system and excommunicated from public worship—not even their offerings were acceptable. Simon was a zealot—a political fanatic—as was James the Younger. And it is thought likely that Judas Iscariot was also a member of the explosive zealot group. Phillip was apparently more respectable than the rest but was an avowed pessimist.

The original Twelve were a diverse and unlikely lot. Given the chance, you and I would not have picked them to be friends or members of our church committees. Yet, all but one turned out to be effective and devoted leaders in the Jesus movement. In fact, someone has wisely said that the group of rugged individualistic men, some devout women, and assorted folks from the fringes of society became so transformed because of their friendship with Jesus that they turned the first-century world upside down. We ask: What made the difference? It was their intimate relationship with Christ and devotion to each other as friends. These people gave us a relationship model and a mission for spiritual living that will serve us well as we move into the twenty-first century.

Very briefly, I want to refer to another friendship model in the Bible drama. At an early stage in the lead character in this friendship saga was a man known to us as Barnabas, a feature actor who appears in the very heart of the Book of Acts. Actually, his name was Joseph, and although he was a Jew, he was a native of Cyprus, an island in the northeastern corner of the Mediterranean Sea. Joseph was an early convert to Christianity and had become a member of the church in Jerusalem. It was there he was given the surname of Barnabas—a word that in Hebrew means "son of encouragement" (Acts 4:36).

Barnabas moved to center stage in the Acts story with the arrival in Jerusalem of Saul of Tarsus, who we also know as Paul, the Greek version of his name. We know that after Paul's confrontation with Christ on the Damascus road, he went into seclusion for an extended period of time. Later he traveled to Jerusalem, undoubtedly to identify with and be accepted by the Christians there, but they rejected his overtures out of fear. After all, they remembered well this same Saul, a rigid Pharisee, who had not too long before persecuted any believer in Jesus that he could track down—no Christian had been safe from his bitter and ruthless attacks. There was just no way they were able to believe his story and accept him. But

Barnabas befriended Paul, believed his story, and vouched for him so that he was finally accepted into the Christian community. After that, though, we read that Paul left Jerusalem and returned to his home city of Tarsus.

In the meantime, Christianity was spreading rapidly out from Palestine, and a strong community of believers was formed in the Syrian city of Antioch. Barnabas was sent by the Jerusalem church to shepherd these new Christians, but soon he needed more help and support. So Barnabas left Antioch and traveled north to Tarsus in search of his friend Paul. After an extensive hunt Barnabas located Paul, whom he persuaded to accompany him back to Antioch, and they worked together in this church where believers in the Way were first called Christians.

During this time together Barnabas probably exerted a profound influence on Paul's thinking and his understanding of the Christian faith and message. It is obvious that their friendship ripened, because we soon find the two of them working and traveling together on a missionary trip to the island of Cyprus and then on to Asia Minor under the sponsorship of the Antioch Christians. While this was a relatively short trip, they were able to establish a number of new churches. It was a successful trip, even though young John Mark, who had started out with them, turned back and returned home before they had gone too far. Apparently John Mark's leaving was very irksome to Paul.

Barnabas and Paul hadn't been home long after that first trip before they decided to start out again and visit the churches they had established earlier and then extend their efforts to communities they had not visited before. This time, however, the two friends had a strong disagreement. Barnabas wanted to give his young cousin John Mark a second chance and take him with them, but Paul strongly disagreed because he had deserted them on the first trip. To Paul, John Mark was a quitter and did not deserve a second chance. Because of this difference of opinion, the two men decided to separate. Paul took another companion on the trip with him, and Barnabas, still the friendly mentor and encourager, took John Mark and went off in another direction.

We have only the bare bones of the story, but I don't think it stretches our imaginations too much to picture Barnabas as seeing that Paul was now well established in the faith and didn't need him as much as he had before. On the other hand, young John Mark sorely needed the friendship and guidance of his older cousin at this crisis time of his life.

Once again, Barnabas—the "son of encouragement" —was a mentor and friend to one who needed his support and guidance. Even as his friendship with Saul of Tarsus (Paul) had produced a vibrant and energetic Christian witness and an encourager of Christians, new and established, now Barnabas shifted his influence to another promising young man. A future isolated reference and early tradition places John Mark in positions of church leadership and credits him with being the author of what we know as the Gospel of Mark. Additional tradition credits John Mark with being the first to preach the Good News of Jesus Christ in Egypt and of being the founder of the large and influential Christian community in Alexandria.

What a marvelous heritage of friendship this man Barnabas has passed along to us. For we are all called to be sons and daughters of encouragement to people along the way. Someone has wisely said that we cannot be Christians in a vacuum. Most certainly, we need each other to be all that God wants us to be. Author Scott Peck, in his bestselling book entitled *The Road Less Traveled*, states that love is "the will to extend one's self for the purpose of nurturing one's own or another's spiritual growth."[3] That is a true expression of the gift of friendship.

Several years ago a man named Allen Emory, longtime associate of Billy Graham, wrote a delightful book entitled *Turtle on a Fencepost*.[4] According to Allen Emory, many years ago a person would at times come across an unusual sight while walking down a country lane in New England —a turtle would be perched right on top of a fencepost. One thing you could know for sure was that there was just no way that turtle could have gotten up there by himself. Someone had to stoop down, pick up the turtle, and set him on his fencepost perch.

The point of the illustration and the book was simply this: We are all turtles on the fenceposts of our lives. Over the years friends and mentors have had confidence in us and have given us the lift and encouragement necessary to be where we are. At the same time, each of us is called upon to exercise our gift of friendship and lift up and encourage others so they can be all that God wants them to be.

In reflecting on the Barnabas story and the turtle-on-the-fencepost parable, my thoughts have floated back over the years to a couple of people whose gift of friendship has been a powerful and sustaining force to me. The first was just a little girl when I first knew her. It was shortly after Roy and I were married, and we were living in Hollywood. Our two children, Cheryl and Linda, had become friends with two little neighborhood girls.

Judy, one of the little girls, became almost like a daughter to me. Her family didn't attend church, but she became interested and began attending Fountain Avenue Baptist Church with us, and after a time she accepted Christ as her Savior. Over the many years since that time, Judy has remained a fast friend and has stood by me during times of heartbreak and tragedy. For example, when our Debbie was killed in the 1964 bus accident and Roy was confined to a hospital because of a spinal fusion, it was Judy who spent the long and painful night with me. When I had my heart attack on May 10, 1992, she visited me regularly in Loma Linda Medical Center, and I knew she was praying constantly for me.

Another close friend, Marguerite Hamilton, shared my heartbreak in 1950 when our Robin came into the world as a Down's syndrome baby. I had met Marguerite and her wonderful daughter Nancy just shortly before Robin was born. Nancy's hands and feet were badly deformed, and she was one of the sweetest children I have ever known. All through Robin's two years in this world, Marguerite and Nancy were a great consolation to me. Although both Robin and Nancy have gone on to be with their heavenly Father, Marguerite has remained a close and supportive friend over these many years.

Through God's marvelous provision of the gift of friendship, I have been made stronger over the years by Roy and my family and by a great host of friends. They have given me strength for today and hope for all of the tomorrows to come.

Dorothy Baird, another staunch Christian friend, beautifully expressed my deepest feelings in her poem "Forever Friends."

Friends who know us and yet love us
are often hard to find.
They share in our sadness;
They help bring us gladness
and continue to be so kind.

Whether separated by miles,
    or daily sharing smiles,
We remain true friends of the heart.
We meet, hug, and talk.
Share a meal, take a walk
    as though we've never been apart.
Our faults, they forgive us;
Our problems they share with us.
They're generous with compassion and love.
Not just friends in the sunshine,
    but friends through a lifetime;
They're sent from the Lord above.
Thank God for true friends
    whose love never ends. . . .
Those special, forever friends.

7

Say Yes to
GOD'S GIFT OF RISK
AND DIFFICULTY

*Inevitably, living the Christian life is a risky
adventure—one pregnant with difficulties.
But for the Christian, Jesus reminds us, "In the
world you have trouble [risk and difficulties].
But take heart! I have overcome the world."*

Olaf M. Norlie

*I*n George Bernard Shaw's play *Saint Joan* there is a powerful statement about the risk and danger in our faith and
Christian pilgrimage. Before sentence was passed on Joan
of Arc, Bishop Cauchin said to her, "My child, you are in
love with religion." In response Joan asked, "I never
thought of that; is there any harm in it?" To which the
bishop answered, "No, my child. There is no harm in it.
But there is danger."

Today, we are inclined to think that the risk and danger of being a Christian dates back to the fifteenth-century world of Joan of Arc. Yet in 1980 the civilized world was shocked at the death of four missionaries in El Salvador. As I write this in late 1992, the newspapers headline the tragic story of five Catholic nuns from Illinois who were killed in a suburb of Monrovia, Liberia.

Most of us, though, are not risking our lives as Christians. Nevertheless, if we are faithful to our commitment to Christ, there are other subtle forms of risk that threaten us. True, we think of risk, difficulties, and dangers as being threats, but as I've thought about God's provisions for our growth and spiritual health, I have come to believe that risk is one of God's gifts—as painful as it may be at times.

In the recent past there has been an epidemic of criticism directed toward members of the United States Congress and accompanied by a kind of raw cynicism. It is true, of course, that there are those who have flagrantly abused their power and privileges, betraying the trust their constituents have placed in them. This sort of thing has been going on since the days of the ancient city-states in the Middle East.

However, since the forming of our government in the late eighteenth century, our Congress and national leadership have been made up of men and women of principle who were—and are—willing to risk their political reputations by adhering to their convictions. Many of these have been and are committed Christians.

Among them is an old friend of ours, the Honorable Mark O. Hatfield, the senior senator from the state of Oregon. Several years ago Senator Hatfield wrote a book titled *Between a Rock and a Hard Place*. In it he recounted numerous incidents in which his Christian convictions clashed with what would seem to be politically expedient. For him, these were times of painful risk.

Of the several stories Senator Hatfield told, one especially piqued my interest. The time was early 1973. Senator John Stennis of Mississippi asked Senator Hatfield to speak briefly to the National Presidential Prayer Breakfast in Washington, D.C., on behalf of the Senate Prayer Group. At the time discussions and feelings about the American action in Vietnam were at a fever pitch, and it was widely known that Mark Hatfield, out of strong Christian conviction, was personally opposed to the government policy at the time.

After wrestling with whether or not to accept Senator Stennis's invitation and after consulting with friends and associates from whom he received conflicting advice, Senator Hatfield decided to honor the invitation of his friend. In doing so he was reminded that among the three thousand guests at the prayer breakfast would be the president and other national leaders. "My intention," he wrote, "was to say some word which would be relevant to them, and faithful to my own convictions; to give a faithful witness to truth and to my Lord."

Senator Hatfield arrived at the meeting that morning and took his seat at the head table. "I began to sense the tension growing inside me," he wrote. "My long-time friend Billy Graham was seated next to me on my left; President Nixon was on my right. Cabinet officers and other members of the Congress were all nearby. I could not help but think, am I going to make a fool of myself before all these friends and associates? It was that feeling we all know which bids us to go along with the crowd, or not to risk doing something that may displease people whose friendship we deeply value. These thoughts and feelings flashed through me."

The full text of Senator Hatfield's remarks offered a thoughtful and respectful statement of his feelings. A short yet moving excerpt merits our attention. The Senator said, "We sit here today as the wealthy and powerful. But let us not forget that those who follow Christ will more often find themselves not with the comfortable majorities, but with the miserable minorities. Today our prayers must begin with repentance. Individually, we must ask forgiveness for the exile of love from our hearts. And corporately as a people, we must turn in repentance from the sin that scarred our national soul." He closed with these words, "We must continually be transformed by Jesus Christ and take his commands seriously. Let us be Christ's messengers of reconciliation and peace, giving our lives over to the power of his love. Then we can soothe the wounds of war, and renew the face of the earth and all mankind."

During Senator Hatfield's remarks, he caught the hostile looks of certain leadership people. In the days that followed it became clear that even though he had made no direct mention of the Vietnam war or the president that there were those who interpreted the incident "as a direct confrontation with the President."[1]

Throughout Mark Hatfield's long political career—first as a representative in the Oregon State Legislature, then as a state senator, a two-term governor of Oregon, and a United States senator since 1966—he has placed his reputation and career in jeopardy as often as necessary in obedience to what he believed was God's will for his life. The response to the risks involved is the ongoing respect of both those who have agreed with him and those who have disagreed.

Roy and I have usually been good risk takers. Two incidents in particular stand out in my mind. The setting for the first incident was in New York City. Just three weeks after our little Robin died, we were scheduled for an appearance in Madison Square Garden. The show had been booked two years before, and we felt we should keep the date even though our feelings were raw from the loss of our loved one.

In planning for the show Roy decided that he wanted to sing "Peace in the Valley," because it was the Lord's peace and sustaining grace that was enabling us to go through with the commitment. The song was—and is—a great favorite of Roy's, and he wanted its witness to be felt by everyone in attendance.

After we arrived at the Garden, Roy and the Sons of the Pioneers worked up a beautiful arrangement of "Peace in the Valley." Roy then made arrangements with the light crew to darken the Garden at a certain place in the song and throw a lighted cross on the turf by means of special lighting.

At the dress rehearsal everything went off beautifully. When Roy reached that place in the song, "the lion will lay down with the lamb," the house went dark and the lighted cross was brilliant against the dark turf. It was most effective. Immediately after the rehearsal, however, the Garden management called us to the front office and said, "You cannot show that cross in this show. You'll have to take it out."

Roy looked the manager right in the eye and said, "No, that cross has a special meaning for us at this time. The cross stays in." In response the manager said, "Impossible. You cannot do it." And with that Roy said, "Then get yourself another cowboy. Dale and I are going back to California." The Garden management hadn't expected this, so they finally gave in and agreed the lighted cross effect could stay in.

Our first performance was an afternoon matinee, and the balcony was full of teenagers from parochial schools on Long Island. When Roy reached that climax in "Peace in the Valley" and the cross appeared on the floor of the darkened Garden, those young people jumped to their feet and cheered with a deafening roar of approval. That convinced the Garden management, and the cross stayed in for all of the remaining performances. The risk Roy took paid off. When we risk for God, he *will* honor our efforts.

The second incident occurred when we were invited by the Billy Graham Association to participate in the first London Crusade. Since we had not been there before, we planned to arrive ahead of time and do a tour of several of the major cities in England, Scotland, and Ireland. The British producer arranged for these appearances because at that time the British Roy Rogers fan club was the largest one in the world.

For the Glasgow appearance we decided that after our regular program we would do a little salute to God and country. I mentioned how important the Bible was to us and that we were in this part of the world to participate in the Billy Graham Crusade, and I urged the people to go down and hear him. We then closed out the evening by singing "God Save the Queen" and "How Great Thou Art."

When word got to the producer about our little addition to the secular show, he called Art Rush on the telephone and said, "We didn't hire those people to preach. We hired them to entertain. Tell Dale Evans to quit talking about God and Billy Graham." I told Art everything would stay just as it was, and we then went ahead in spite of the producer's complaints.

Before our scheduled Belfast appearance, the producer called Art and told him to warn me that those Irish Catholics would probably throw garbage at me if I boosted the Graham meetings. I went ahead anyway, and at the conclusion of the program we were given a standing ovation—the only time that happened on the entire tour. Then as I was about to leave, one of the ushers came up and told me that someone wanted to see me in the wings.

My visitor was a lovely Irish monk who identified himself as the chaplain of the Abbey Players. Then he said, "I wanted to ask you a very personal question; I hope you will answer it for me. What kind of a man is Billy Graham?" I said, "Sir, he is the most utterly consecrated Christian that I have ever had the privilege of knowing." With that, he extended his hand, took mine, and said, "I knew it." Once again, the risk had produced positive results—God is always faithful!

As I've thought about these risk stories, I have been reminded of that parade of biblical people who took formidable risks. One of them is an unnamed woman; the writer of both the Gospel of Mark and the Gospel of Luke tell her story. In setting the scene the Gospel writers picture Jesus walking down the street in the middle of a crushing crowd.

In that crowd was a desperate woman who had suffered with a hemorrhage for twelve years. This was apparently a common illness at that time, and Jewish lore specified at least eleven cures for the debilitating ailment—some were obviously quack remedies, while others had a reasonable chance of success. We are told, though, that nothing had helped this woman in spite of the fact that doctor bills had wiped her out financially.

When she saw Jesus in the crowd, she knew that he was the one who had become famous in Galilee as a healer. So she decided on the spur of the moment to take a risk—she would slip up behind him unobtrusively and touch the fringe on the bottom of his robe with the hope that she would be healed. Such a brazen action was an outrageous intrusion because her illness, according to Jewish law, made her ceremonially unclean. This simply meant that anything or anyone she touched would also be unclean. Then, too, there was the risk of discovery, but she decided to take the chance. It isn't hard to picture the scene as she slipped up behind Jesus, bent over when no one was looking, and gingerly touched the fringe of his robe.

At that moment, though, her world fell apart, for Jesus whirled around and asked, "Who touched my clothes?" In understandable amazement Jesus' disciples said, "You see the crowd pressing in on you; how can you say, 'Who touched me?' "Then in embarrassment and fear the woman identified herself—she was the guilty person. With this admission, Jesus assured her that she was healed, and he told her that her faith had made her well. She had met Jesus, and it was worth the risk. (See Mark 5:25–34; Luke 8:43–48.)

Among the many risk takers in the Bible drama is another very unlikely character—Nicodemus. He appears in just two scenes, but both are highly significant. First, we encounter Nicodemus, a proud Pharisee and a distinguished member of the Jewish Council, talking with Jesus under cover of darkness. Even under those circumstances, he was risking a great deal if he was caught talking to this subversive teacher. The super-religious Pharisees and the Temple hierarchy labeled Jesus a heretic and a disturber of the peace. To be sympathetic with him was to invite trouble and harassment.

Nicodemus decided, as did the woman in the crowd, that the encounter was worth the risk. For it was to Nicodemus that Jesus said, "No one can see the kingdom of God without being born from above." And it was to Nicodemus that Jesus spoke these immortal words, "For God so loved the world that he gave his only Son, so that everyone who believes in him may not perish but may have eternal life" (John 3:3, 16).

The second scene with Nicodemus finds him taking an enormous risk as he joins Joseph from the village of Arimathea in removing Jesus from the cross and burying his body in the Garden Tomb. (See John 19:39–42.) We can gather from this bold action that for this once proud and self-righteous Pharisee the risk has been worth it, for it is obvious that he had indeed been "born from above" and was no longer skittish about being recognized as a follower of the Galilean.

While we're looking at risk takers in our New Testament drama, we don't dare overlook Zacchaeus. The scene for this delightful story was the city of Jericho, a bustling center on an important east-west highway. It was a rich community of balsam groves and date palms that were owned largely by King Herod and the royal family.

Zacchaeus was probably the chief tax collector in Jericho and was a man of considerable wealth. Apparently he had heard that the Galilean preacher and healer would be passing through town on his way to Jerusalem. Curiosity got the best of Zacchaeus, and since he was a short man and was unable to see over the taller folks who lined the street, he risked looking foolish, climbed up a tree, and shinnied out onto a limb that hung over the crowded street. Certain that he wouldn't be observed, he felt comfortable in spite of his awkward perch.

Wonder of wonders, when Jesus reached a spot just below Zacchaeus, he looked up and said, "Zacchaeus, hurry and come down; for I must stay at your house today." With that Zacchaeus risked the ire of the religious authorities and did exactly what Jesus had requested. In fact, we're told that Zacchaeus was "happy to welcome him." The risk of looking foolish and then entertaining an unpopular traveling preacher paid off because of his remarkable conversion and moral turnaround. (See Luke 19:1–10.)

In this marvelous story Zacchaeus got the full treatment. That's the way God works! Author C. S. Lewis understood this well when he gave us this delightful bit of wisdom,

> When I was a child I often had a toothache, and I knew that if I went to my mother she would give me something which would deaden the pain for that night and let me go to sleep. But I did not go to my mother—at least, until the pain became very bad. And the reason I did not go was this. I did not doubt she would give me the aspirin; but I knew she would also do something else. I knew she would take me to the dentist the next morning. I could not get what I wanted out of her without getting something more,

which I did not want. I wanted immediate relief
from pain; but I could not get it without having my
teeth set permanently right. And I knew those den-
tists; I knew they started fiddling about with all sorts
of other teeth which had not yet begun to ache.[2]

To the serious person there is no partial conversion—no quick fix.

As St. Paul discovered, living the Christian life is a risky business. As long as he was a respectable, synagogue-going Pharisee who obeyed the religious rules and fulfilled the rituals, he lived a risk-free and comfortable life. However, after meeting the risen Jesus on the Damascus road and after being converted under the guidance of Ananias, his life from then on was full of risk and danger. Yet it is apparent that it was worth the risk and danger for the great apostle. He testified to this in a letter to his "son" Timothy not long before his death,

I have fought the good fight, I have finished the race,
I have kept the faith. From now on there is reserved
for me the crown of righteousness, which the Lord,
the righteous judge will give me.
　　　　　　　　　　　　[2 Tim. 4:7–8]

Let's face it, though. In spite of what we have learned from such biblical models as the sick woman on the crowded street, Nicodemus, Zacchaeus, and Paul we all strive desperately to lead comfortable, secure, successful, and risk-free lives. We often strive for the understanding of our friends and associates at the expense of taking an unpopular stand that is dictated by our spiritual and moral principles.

There is something more here, however, that seems important. I think we often avoid taking risks because of the fear of failure. Somehow everything about our culture puts a premium on success and a stigma on the possibility of failure, but this doesn't square with the way things work. Recently, I saw a program featuring Mark Goodson, the creator of many top television game shows. The interviewer asked Mr. Goodson what percentage of the shows he had written were successful. After a thoughtful silence he said, "One out of five." That means four out of five wouldn't be classed as successful in today's television world. Isn't it amazing then that Mr. Goodson is great because of the one out of five that are successful?

In 1992 Tom Seaver, pitcher for the New York Mets, was elected to Baseball's Hall of Fame with a win-loss lifetime record of 311-205. He won 311 games, but he lost 205 games—he failed 205 times, but being willing to risk that, Tom Seaver had the enviable record of 311 games won. Yes, the risk of failure is always there, but in the game of life we are to concentrate on the positives.

One thing for sure—in our passion to avoid rocking life's boat and to avoid risk, we miss the stretching experiences of life as God intended it to be when he created us in his image. I just don't believe it was God's intention for us to play it safe and take it easy. Paul Tournier set the mood when he wrote, "My wish for everyone is that they will be jolted from time to time by life, and that they will be faced with the need to make new departures," and he urges us to avoid becoming "prisoners of duty."[3] In his wonder-filled book entitled *The Meaning of Persons*, Dr. Tournier wrote about the adventure of living a rich and meaningful life, "It means accepting risks: 'nothing ventured, nothing won,' says the proverb. We think that by being cautious we are protecting life, whereas we are slowly smothering it. Our Lord's words come to mind: 'Whoever will save his life shall lose it' (Mark 8:35)."[4]

Dr. Alan Jones records a question and answer exchange between the eloquent Jewish writer Elie Wiesel and a questioner: "He was once asked about the difficulty of believing in God after the experience of the Holocaust—is belief possible after Auschwitz? Wiesel responded that if it was hard to live in a world without faith in God, it was even harder to live a life of faith. If you want difficulties, choose to live with God."[5]

As Christians we need to be reminded daily that the symbol of Christianity is not a padded rocking chair, nor a dollar sign in the bank book, nor a paid-up health care plan. No, the symbol of Christianity that is recognized around the world is the cross. Remember, the miracle of

Easter morning was made possible by the cross.

Most certainly, even a sketchy look at the life of Jesus when he was here on earth reflects a life of risk from the human point of view. From the beginning of his life of public service at Cana in Galilee to his crucifixion and death on Golgotha outside the walls of Jerusalem, Jesus risked his life in the fulfillment of his earthly destiny. All of this made possible the Easter miracle of his resurrection. Then after his return to the Father, his disciples and early followers risked their lives again and again in making the Good News available to people everywhere.

Author John Knox expressed it well when he wrote, "The primitive Christian community was not a memorial society with its eyes fastened on a departing master; it was a dynamic community created around a living and present Lord."[6]

Those first- and second-century Christians modeled for us in an unforgettable way the risk involved in living the life of faith. It wasn't easy, and their very lives were frequently on the line, but they said *Yes* to God's gift of risk and moved on to change the world. For them and for us, the game of life involves moving boldly to accept this gift from the Lord as we make our way each hour of the day.

In his *The Miracle of Easter*, Floyd Thatcher wrote, "An unidentified war correspondent in a rare moment of inspiration wrote these moving lines:

Some men die by shrapnel,
Some go down in flames.
But most men perish inch by inch
Who play at little games.

The Miracle of Easter points to a lifestyle not of medioc-
rity and littleness but to one of 'big games.' It involves
risk and venturing and change as we move toward the
wholeness which God has designed for each of us."[7]

Say Yes to
GOD'S GIFT OF FAITH

*The life of faith is not a life of mounting up with
wings, but a life of walking and not fainting. . . .
Faith never knows where it is being led,
but it loves and knows the one who is leading.*

Oswald Chambers

*Faith can only originate in the soul of man
by the gift of God.*

Marcus L. Loane

*E*arly morning in our high desert home near Victorville,
California, is my special time of being alone with the
Lord. There's a clean aroma in the invigorating morning
air, and the birds nesting in our trees sing their approval
of the bright new morning. As I look out across the vastness
of the rolling hills dotted with yucca and other desert

plants and flowers, I am reminded of the psalmist's reaction to a comparable scene in Judah,

> *This is the day that the LORD has made;*
> *let us rejoice and be glad in it.*

[Ps. 118:24]

In another place the sacred writer, in a moment of what I like to think was celebration of the early morning, was inspired to write these words,

> *The winter is past,*
> *the rains are over and gone;*
> *the flowers appear in the countryside;*
> *the time is coming when the birds will sing,*
> *and the turtle-dove's cooing will be heard in our land.*

[Song of Sol. 2:11–12 NEB]

Somehow there is a special magic in mornings like this as I sit with a cup of coffee at my elbow and my Bible in my lap. God seems especially close, and the words of another psalm writer take on a moving and intensely personal feeling,

> *The heavens are telling the glory of God;*
> *and the firmament proclaims his handiwork.*

[Ps. 19:1]

Such moments are times of celebration for me as I affirm once again my faith in God—a faith that has sustained me through the pain and death of loved ones and my more recent heart attack. I have come to understand more clearly that faith is not a sense, nor a sight, nor reason, but a taking of God at his word.

I have a love for God's great and beautiful outdoors that had its beginning in the wide-open spaces of my childhood home in central Texas and has come to a deeply satisfying maturity in our California desert home. Because of that love I find it easy to identify with David, the psalmist, whose faith gives me powerful support for each day.

Much of David's life, especially those years before he was crowned king of Israel, was spent in the Judean hill country tending his father's herds of sheep under all sorts of weather conditions. There he would have experienced the dampness of the early morning dew as the black sky turned to gray and the sun edged up over the eastern hills. There, too, he would have watched the storm clouds roll in from the western sea and unload sheets of rain with the roar of thunder and the blinding zigzag of lightning.

Yes, I can identify with David as he accepted God's gift of faith when he saw God in the awesome wonders of his great and wonderful world. David's earthy faith shines brightly in the Bible narrative of his time, but three of his psalm-poems especially have enriched my own gift of faith: Psalms 27, 37, and 57.

First is the great affirmation,

> *The LORD is my light and my salvation;*
> *whom shall I fear?*
> *The LORD is the stronghold of my life;*
> *of whom shall I be afraid?*

[Ps. 27:1]

Then as David moves toward the close and climax of this magnificent psalm, we hear him saying,

> *My God does hear when I cry out to him. He does*
> *not ignore my needs, nor is he indifferent to my*
> *desires. He will not let me go even if my very own*
> *family should turn against me. He will sustain me*
> *and keep me on course through the dangers and*
> *pitfalls of this life. It is possible to know and*
> *experience God's love in this uncertain, tumultuous*
> *existence. Take courage, step out in faith, scorning*
> *consequences. Let God have his way with you.*[1]

This twenty-seventh Psalm was a powerful faith document for David Jacobsen, director of the American University of Beirut's Medical Center, during his seventeen torturous months as a hostage held by the Hizballah, the dreaded archfundamentalist Muslim terrorists. Mr. Jacobsen's ordeal began on May 28, 1985, when he was abducted at gunpoint on a Beirut street, forced into a van, clubbed by his kidnappers' gun butt, and spirited away.

Mr. Jacobsen's months of captivity are a horror story that is almost unbelievable in an otherwise civilized world. But in his remarkable book entitled *Hostage,* he writes, "I made the twenty-seventh Psalm a credo for my survival, 'The Lord is my light and my salvation. Whom shall I fear?' I would not be frightened by Hizballah. I should fear only that I might lose my values, my faith. 'One thing I have desired of the Lord, that I should seek: That I may dwell in the house of the Lord all the days of my life.' If I resolved to make my cell the house of the Lord, then I could survive the ordeal."[2]

Next in our David story, we see that his faith comes through with brilliant certainty in the poetic beauty of Psalm 37. Here David's faith takes shape as he says,

> *Trust in the LORD, and do good . . . .*
> *Take delight in the LORD*
>   *and he will give you the desires of your heart.*
> *Commit your way to the LORD;*
>   *trust in him, and he will act.*
> *Be still before the LORD,*
>   *and wait patiently for him.*

[Ps. 37:3–5, 7]

Drawing on a modern translation, we hear David as he continues, "God has not taken a vacation; he is here. . . . It will take time, but the victory is ultimately God's. Those who live in God's will shall surely discover that his purposes prevail, that true joy and peace and security come from him. Let us wait on God and seek daily to obey him. He is our salvation and our security, and nothing in this world can take that away from us."[3]

It is generally believed that these words were written while David was a fugitive from King Saul, yet his trust and faith are firmly fixed on his ever-present God. How grateful we can be that God is never on vacation.

In the early words of Psalm 57 we sense that David is still on the run as a fugitive. Even though he knows that Saul has a contract out on his life, the closing words of the psalm reflect David's faith, "Your love, O God, is steadfast; Your grace is everlasting. Even when I'm beaten down by depression and ensnared by my weakness and frailties and my own lust threatens to devour me, you are my God and you will not let me go. I am determined to serve you, O Lord. May my life be a continual thank offering to you. I shall sing your praises forever."[4]

The key word in David's psalm of praise is *steadfast*— faithful, determined. It is this kind of faith the apostle Paul had in mind when he wrote to his Christian friends in Corinth, "Therefore, my beloved, be steadfast, immovable, always excelling in the work of the Lord, because you know that in the Lord your labor is not in vain" (1 Cor. 15:58).

The inspired writer of the First Epistle of John caught the spirit of David's faith when he gave us these words, "All of us who are born of God are gaining the victory over the world. It is our faith which gives us the victory."[5]

Another inspiring faith role model moved onto the stage of our biblical story many years before King David's time. Her name was Ruth, the central character in one of the most beautifully crafted short stories in all literature. Ruth was the great-grandmother of David and one of the four women listed in Matthew's genealogy of Jesus.

There are a number of reasons why I find the drama of Ruth a faith challenge. We first meet her in her native land of Moab, and are introduced to her as the wife of one of the sons of a widow named Naomi—Israelite refugees from Judah. According to the story, the wife of Naomi's other son was named Orpah, also a native of Moab.

After several years, both of Naomi's sons had died. This meant that Naomi, Ruth, and Orpah were alone. When Naomi decided to return to her homeland of Judah, her two daughters-in-law started to accompany her. Apparently they had gone just a little way when Naomi, knowing the emotional upheaval of being a stranger in a foreign country, urged Ruth and Orpah to remain in their native land so they could put the pieces of their lives together again in company with their friends and relatives.

According to the storyteller, Orpah did return to her home, but Ruth insisted on staying with her mother-in-law. That is the last we hear of Orpah, but according to certain Jewish legends, Orpah was the great-great-grandmother of the giant Goliath who terrorized the Israelite army when the Philistines and the Israelites were poised for battle in the valley of Elah. Obviously, we have no proof of the intriguing possibility, but we do know for a fact that Ruth was David's great-grandmother, and we do have the colorful story of David's winning contest over Goliath.

We know from the story that Ruth continued west with Naomi, and the two women made their home among Naomi's old friends and kinfolk in Bethlehem. We know, too, that Ruth abandoned her Moabite gods and put faith in the true God of Israel. After a fascinating chain of events, she married one of Bethlehem's leading citizens, a man named Boaz. In due course Ruth had a son named Obed, the father of Jesse, the father of David the psalmist and Israel's king.

It was Ruth's love for her mother-in-law and her faith in God that held her steady in a foreign land among strange people. And it was Ruth's faith that enabled her to not only make a new life but to become an important figure in Israel's history—important enough, in fact, to be listed as one of Jesus' ancestors, even though she was not a Jew.

More than once as I've traveled in foreign countries where the customs and language are far different from what I understand, I have marveled at the quality of

Ruth's love and her implicit faith in a God who accepted her as she was and used her in the fulfillment of his salvation plans.

David's God, Ruth's God, and former hostage David Jacobsen's God is a far cry from the story C. S. Lewis tells about the schoolboy who was asked what he thought God was like. He replied that "as far as he could make out, God was 'the sort of person who is always snooping round to see if anyone is enjoying himself and then trying to stop it.' "[6]

No, the God who has made possible the gift of faith is no snoop or joy-killer. Rather he is the God who is *for* us; the God who so loved us "that he gave his only Son, so that everyone who believes in him may not perish but may have eternal life" (John 3:16).

Pope John Paul II has become a stalwart symbol of faith to Christians—Protestant and Catholic—all over the world. I like this brief message he has given us about faith: "In faith we find the victory that overcomes the world. Because we are united with Jesus and sustained by him, there is no challenge we cannot meet, no difficulty we cannot sustain, no obstacle we cannot overcome for the Gospel. Indeed Christ himself guarantees that 'he who believes in me will also do the works that I do; and greater works than these he will do.' The answer to so many problems is found only in faith—a faith manifested and sustained in prayer."[7]

In spite of these reassurances, we all have our moments when our stream of faith seems to have dried up—when it seems as if our faith is far too small to handle the staggering problems that confront us each day. At such moments I find reassurance in the words of Jesus, "I tell you the truth, *if you have faith as small as a mustard seed,* you can say to this mountain, 'Move from here to there' and it will move. Nothing will be impossible for you" (Matt. 17:20 NIV, italics mine.) What wonderful good news!

In these words Jesus used an example very familiar to his listeners. They knew all about mustard seeds and just how little they were. So then Jesus told them—and us— that if we exercise just a little bit, just a speck, of his abundant gift of faith, we can move mountains. *Moving mountains* was a Jewish expression for beating or grinding into powder one's difficulties—reducing them to nothing. As if that wasn't enough, Jesus went on to say that with mustard-seed-sized-faith, nothing is impossible— we can do anything!

Faith is a gift from God, and it is ours to nurture, for as we use it, it will grow. Most certainly, the apostle Paul caught the drift of what Jesus had said about faith when he gave this witness to his brothers and sisters in Christ at the church in Philippi in northern Greece, "I can do all things through Christ which strengtheneth me" (Phil. 4:13 KJV).

In one of his sermons, Dr. Norman Vincent Peale said that these seven words can change your life—"I can do all things through Christ." Dr. Peale went on to say, "If you really get going with those seven words, *really* meaning it, *really* believing it, *really* practicing it; and if anything that isn't good in your life is cast out, your life can be changed."[8]

Patrick Henry was one of the great heroes of the American Revolution. He was also the gifted orator who stood up in the little white church in Richmond, Virginia, and gave his famous "Give me liberty or give me death" speech. Of even greater importance, though, was the fact that Patrick Henry had received the gift of faith, a faith he cherished above all else. These are his words, "My most cherished possession I wish I could leave you is my faith in Jesus Christ, for with him and nothing else you can be happy, but without him and with all else you'll never be happy."

In a similar way my mother's faith is a most cherished possession of mine. From the time when I first accepted Jesus as my Savior at the age of ten until I was an adult of thirty-five, my mother prayed that I would really turn my life completely over to the Lord. Those were wavering and wondering years for me. The day came, though, when my decision was made, and I gave myself fully and without reservation to God. At that moment the Lord vindicated my mother's faith in answer to her prayers and those of my son and friends. I am so glad that my mother lived to see the results of her faith.

Unfortunately, from a human point of view it doesn't always work that way. When I think of my maternal grandmother, Mama Wood, I'm reminded of the Bible's definition of faith as given to us by the writer of the Book of Hebrews, "Now faith is the assurance of things hoped for, the conviction of things not seen" (Heb 11:1). For many years Mama Wood prayed that her son, my Uncle Roy, would accept Christ as his Savior.

When World War II plunged our world into a fiery conflagration, Uncle Roy was sent overseas without Mama Wood seeing the answer to her prayers. Her faith was unwavering, however, and she gave herself to the work of her church, the First Baptist Church of Uvalde, Texas. Her witness for Christ influenced many people, and while her faith remained firm, she died while Uncle Roy was overseas. What she had "hoped for" with Uncle Roy was "not seen."

When the war was over and Uncle Roy came home, his first act was to attend church. It was then he accepted Christ, and for the rest of his life he was a dedicated Christian and an active churchman. Mama Wood's faith was fully justified. God never fails, and we can rest easy in the words of Paul to the Christians in Rome and to Christians in all of time, "We know that all things work together for good for those who love God, who are called according to his purpose" (Rom. 8:28).

Say Yes to
GOD'S GIFT OF HOPE

What oxygen is to the lungs,
such is hope for the meaning of life.

Emil Brunner

Our friend Bruce Larson, eloquent pastor and author, several years ago spent a week doing some research at the world-famous Menninger Foundation in Topeka, Kansas. During the course of his various conversations with the Menninger staff, he asked them to identify the most important ingredient in the treatment of their emotionally disturbed patients. "I was told," Bruce Larson writes, "that the entire staff was unanimous in singling out *hope* as the most important factor in treatment. They went on to confess that they don't really know how to give hope to a patient. It is a spiritual and elusive gift."[1]

For those of you who are baseball fans, the name of Casey Stengel, for many years the resourceful manager of the New York Yankees, is legendary. His colorful career has produced many delightful stories and sayings, but I think the most distinctive and descriptive comment ever made about him is this: "He was on good terms with hope." Casey Stengel said *Yes* to hope because he constantly carried with him a vision of a better tomorrow.

Perhaps some of the most electrifying stories of the power of hope to come out of the twentieth century are told by and about prisoners who survived the German concentration camps in the Second World War. Dr. Viktor Frankl, one of Europe's most eminent psychiatrists, was a longtime prisoner in these bestial camps. His father, mother, brother, and wife died in the camps or were victims of the gas ovens. Viktor Frankl, prisoner number 119104, somehow managed to survive even the horrors of Auschwitz.

Dr. Frankl's writings and lectures abound with stories of camp inmates who lost all hope of survival and died while others, one way or another, kept their dreams of a future alive. He insists that any prisoner who lost faith in the future was doomed: "With his loss of belief in the future, he also lost his spiritual hold; he let himself decline and became subject to mental and physical decay." Dr . Frankl adds, "Those who know how close the connection is between the state of mind of a man—his courage and hope, or lack of them—and the state of immunity of his body will understand that the sudden loss of hope and courage can have a deadly affect."[2]

I have to believe that in God's marvelous plan of creation he bestowed upon all people in all of time his gift of hope. It is part of our human condition, but it is up to us to accept and nurture it so it becomes a central fact of our lives.

I remember so well a particular night in my own experience. I had just arrived at the Los Angeles airport on my way home from a speaking engagement. After picking up my car, I headed east toward the mountains I had to cross before reaching Victorville and our home. I hadn't gone far before I was caught in a driving rainstorm. By the time I got into the mountains, the rain was coming down in slanting sheets. Then, without warning, my windshield wipers stopped working. I couldn't see much of anything then, but I managed to ease over onto the shoulder and put on my warning blinkers.

A steady stream of traffic eased past slowly, but nobody stopped. After several minutes of helpless waiting, I pulled on my all-weather coat and climbed out of the car, hoping to flag somebody down. But it didn't work, and I was getting soaked, so I climbed back into the car determined to sit there all night if I had to. I prayed,

"Lord, you promised that you'd never leave or forsake me. Now, I just hope you'll be with me no matter how long I have to wait."

A few minutes later a car pulled up beside me, and I heard a man's voice, "May I help you?" I shouted back above the nose of the storm, "I sure hope so. My windshield wipers don't work, and I can't see a thing." With that, a young Mexican man pulled his car off the road, got out, and walked over to where I was sitting. Roy had told me that if I ever had car trouble when I was alone to never get out and not let anybody inside my car, so I was edgy when this young man opened the car door and climbed in. After examining the wipers, he told me that the wiper battery was dead. He then suggested that I lock the car and ride with him into Palmdale where I could phone Roy for help. This seemed to be the only solution, and by this time I felt at ease with him. When we reached Palmdale and the Holiday Inn, my new-found friend let me out, refusing payment for his kindness, and drove off. While waiting for Roy to arrive, I sat quietly and thanked the Lord. Once again I had been assured that if I placed my trust and hope in the Lord, he would hear and answer.

While collecting my thoughts on God's wonderful gift of hope, I was profoundly impressed by a statement made by Vaclav Havel, a playwright and former president of a free and independent Czechoslovakia. Mr. Havel explained what hope means to him, "I am not an optimist because

I'm not sure that everything ends well, nor am I a pessimist because I'm not sure that everything ends badly! I just carry hope in my heart. Hope is a feeling that life and work have meaning. You either have it or you don't, regardless of the state of the world around you. Life without hope is an empty, boring, and useless life. I cannot imagine that I could strive for something if I did not carry hope in me. I am thankful to God for this gift. It is as big a gift as life itself."

Hope—a vision of the future—has energized people throughout all of history. And from history and the Bible drama we discover some heroic models of people whose lives were invigorated by hope.

History's classical writers have given us rich descriptive accounts of the short life of Alexander the Great, who was born in 356 B.C. Alexander was the son of King Philip of Macedon, and as a pupil of Aristotle, he received the finest education available at that time. After the death of his father, Alexander succeeded to the throne, and in a few short years he gained acclaim as one of the ablest military technicians of the day. The story is told that on the occasion of his leaving Greece for one of his eastern military campaigns he liberally passed out gifts to his friends and associates. So lavish was his generosity that one of his friends said, "Sir, you've given away so much that you'll have nothing left for yourself."To this Alexander responded, "Oh yes, I have. I still have my hopes." Hope and vision for the future burned brightly for Alexander and brought him the fulfillment of his dreams before his untimely death from a burning fever at the age of thirty-three.

We can learn much from Alexander, but we can learn more, I believe, from the many colorful models of hope and courage who are active in the Bible drama. And among them is a young Jewish woman who showed enormous hope and courage in the crisis moments of her life. Her name was Esther, and her story is told in part in the Book of Esther.

Not once in this amazing Esther story is the name of God mentioned, and the words *hope* and *faith* are conspicuously absent. Yet in Esther we have a striking exhibit of hope and trust as she moves, fearfully at times, toward the fulfillment of her destiny.

Esther—Hadassah—an orphaned Jewish girl in exile in the strange land of ancient Persia, was raised by an older cousin named Mordecai. As with most faithful Jews who were a part of a foreign society many miles from Jerusalem, Mordecai and Esther were likely very familiar with the poetry of the ancient psalmists:

> The LORD is my rock,
>   my fortress, and my deliverer.

[Ps. 18:2]

For you, O LORD, are my hope, my trust.

[Ps. 71:5]

Happy are those whose help is the God of Jacob,
Whose hope is in the LORD their God.

[Ps. 146:5]

And it is a good thing they were because, according to the sacred writer, Esther and Mordecai would be put to an earthshaking test. It seems that King Ahasuerus of Persia had deposed his number one queen because she had refused to obey an order, and in doing so she had set a deplorable example for all Persian women. Insubordination of any description could not be tolerated. To replace her, a beauty contest was held to find the most beautiful young woman in all the vast empire of one hundred and twenty-seven provinces stretching from India to Ethiopia.

With a keen eye for beauty—even that of his own cousin—Mordecai entered Esther in the contest. Next we're told that she was judged the most beautiful woman in all the Persian Empire, and that when the king saw her, he immediately fell in love with her and made her his queen. In the apocryphal additions to the Book of Esther, the writer takes us further behind the scenes and gives us Mordecai's instructions to Esther as she prepared to assume her new role, "She was to fear God and keep his commandments just as she had done when she was with him. So Esther made no change in her way of life" (Rest of Esther 2:20 NEB).

After a time, according to the story, jealousy and court intrigue unleashed a plot to kill all of the Jews in the empire because Haman, the prime minister, had a bitter grudge against Mordecai. Through subterfuge Haman got King Ahasuerus to issue an edict that called for all of the Jews to be exterminated on a specified day.

When Mordecai read the edict, in frantic desperation he got word through to Queen Esther that she *must* intervene with the king in order to save not only the lives of thousands of Jews but her own life as well. You see neither King Ahasuerus nor his prime minister knew that the young queen was a Jew, but Mordecai reminded Esther that when her identity was discovered, her life, too, would be in jeopardy.

Esther then reminded her cousin through a note that court protocol prohibited her from going to the throne room without first being invited, and that to do so was at the risk of her life. Mordecai insisted that she chance it, saying, "Perhaps you have come to royal dignity for just such a time as this" (Esther 4:14).

In obedience to all that she hoped and dreamed for her people, Esther decked herself out in all of the splendor of her royal robes and appeared at the door of the king's throne room. Overcome by her manner and beauty, Ahasuerus invited her in and asked what she wanted. In reply, Esther issued an invitation for him and Haman to attend a banquet to be held in her quarters. The king responded to his queen's invitation with enthusiasm.

Esther's banquet must have been a huge success, because during the course of the evening King Ahasuerus asked her to make whatever request she desired and assured her the request would be granted "even to the half of my kingdom" (Esther 5:6). Esther was not ready yet to tip her hand, though, so she issued another invitation for the king and Haman to return the next night for another banquet, and she told them that at that time she would make her request known.

Events unfolded just as Esther had planned, and after the second sumptuous banquet, King Ahasuerus repeated his offer to give Esther whatever she wanted. And this time she bared her soul, and right in front of Haman she revealed his plot to exterminate her and all of her people, the Jews. In a rage the king disposed of Haman and agreed to a plan that would prevent the mass slaughter of the Jews.

Esther, the Jewish queen of Persia, had earned her place in history because of her devotion to the God of Israel. Esther's faith and hope, coupled with her courage, inspire us to be hope-filled Christians in our alien and sometimes precarious world.

To celebrate the deliverance of all of the Jews in Persia and the one hundred and twenty-seven provinces across the ancient near-eastern world that were controlled by the Persian king, the festival of Purim, the most joyous of all Jewish holidays, was established by Mordecai and Esther.

To this day it is celebrated by faithful Jews all around the world one month before Passover. While it is a most joyous and spirited holiday, it has its serious dimension as well for it encourages the Jews to cling to their hopes and never despair in spite of the "Hamans" that may move onto the world scene. The saga of Esther, one of our noblest spiritual ancestors, is an inspiration of hope and courage to God's people in all of time.

In fact, Esther reminds me of how I felt at a time of crisis many years ago. My life wasn't in peril as Esther's was, but I felt my self-esteem and reputation were on the line. The event I am thinking of occurred during the years our television program was on the air.

The producer of our show came to me one day with a problem related to a specific episode in one of the shows. "Dale," he said, "we need a Sunday school kind of chorus for Sherri Jackson [who was a little girl at the time] to sing to her father. We just can't find anything suitable in public domain. Could you write one that would fit into the episode?"

I indicated I was willing to try and asked how much time I had to come up with something. In reply, Jack Lacy said, "Twenty minutes." Completely aghast, I said, "There's just no way I can come up with even the simplest of choruses in just twenty minutes." Quietly Jack responded to my near hysteria, "Try!"

I closed the door of my Samuel Goldwyn Studios dressing room and prayed, "Lord, I have faith in your ability to do anything. Now, you know we need an appropriate little chorus. We desperately need just the right thing to be the kind of witness we want to make. My *hope* and faith are in you. Please give me just the right words and tune."

Suddenly, Paul's words from the thirteenth chapter of First Corinthians flashed into my consciousness—faith, hope, and charity. And wonders of wonders, in twenty minutes' time I had the words and music to "Have Faith, Hope, and Charity, That's the Way to Live Successfully. How Do I Know? The Bible Tells Me So." I tried it out on the cast. They liked it, and we closed the show with it.

When the sponsor and network people saw the show, they said my chorus was too religious, and the producer was instructed to delete it on reruns. However, Don Cornell of the Lucky Strike Hit Parade heard it and asked for permission to record it. It was an immediate hit, and "The Bible Tells Me So" remained on the Hit Parade for weeks. God had his way—my hopes prevailed!

The second model of hope that emerges like a thunder clap from the Bible story is none other than the apostle Paul. In fact, I believe Paul could well be labeled "The Apostle of Hope." To chart Paul's travels and activities throughout all of his life from the moment of his conversion on the Damascus road is to picture years of bone-grinding travel on foot throughout Asia Minor and Greece and by ship on the turbulent waters of the eastern Mediterranean Sea. In those days there was no such thing as first class travel or comfortable hotel accommodations. Paul's land travel involved walking across open country or on the rock-paved Roman roads, and he would have slept out in the open under the stars, plagued by gnats and mosquitoes. But in spite of the hardship, he remained ruggedly determined to travel anywhere and by whatever means possible to share the Good News of salvation through Christ with people who had not heard it before.

Yet there was more. Paul's world was Roman and pagan. The people worshiped a pantheon of gods and goddesses, but in addition they were required to worship the Roman emperor—not to do so was a crime against the state. This simply meant that Paul's message of one God and salvation through Christ only met with official opposition wherever he went.

In writing to his Christian friends in Corinth, Paul called their attention to his beatings and prison experiences:

> *Five times I received from the Jews the forty lashes minus one. Three times I was beaten with rods, once I was stoned, three times I was shipwrecked, I spent a night and a day in the open sea, I have been*

> *constantly on the move. I have been in danger from*
> *rivers, in danger from bandits, in danger from my*
> *own countrymen, in danger from Gentiles....I have*
> *labored and toiled and have often gone without*
> *sleep; I have known hunger and thirst and have*
> *often gone without food; I have been cold and naked.*
>
> [2 Cor. 11:24–27 NIV]

Yet it was this same Paul who ranked hope right along with faith and love as the supreme Christian virtues. (See 1 Cor. 13:13.) This same Paul also sent this marvelous benediction to his Christian friends in the imperial city of Rome, "May the God of hope fill you with all joy and peace by your faith in him, until, by the power of the Holy Spirit, you overflow with hope" (Rom. 15:13 NEB). *Overflow with hope*! That is our calling as Christians as the twentieth century winds down to its last hours. I firmly believe that we are to overflow with hope not as a means of escape from the here and now. Rather, our hope engages us in the concerns and needs of the present.

Yes, the social and political world is in a painful upheaval. As I write more than forty wars are raging in remote areas of planet earth—people are dying from starvation by the thousands and from fiery missiles launched by unknown and known foes. As Christians, though, we are not to be harbingers of pessimism and doom. Rather, we are to celebrate God's gift of hope with joy unspeakable and full of glory.

Dr. Viktor Frankl, who I quoted earlier, said somewhere that "survivors were people who believed they were unfinished with life." Because God's gift of hope, we—you and I—are survivors never finished with life. Hymn-writer and poet Isaac Watts caught the spirit of this when he wrote these electrifying words:

> *O God, our help in ages past,*
> *Our hope for years to come,*
> *Our shelter from the stormy blast,*
> *And our eternal home.*
>
> *O God, our help in ages past,*
> *Our hope for years to come,*
> *Be thou our guide while life shall last,*
> *And our eternal home.*

10

Say Yes to
GOD'S GIFT OF LOVE

*The great tragedy of life
is not that men perish
but that they cease to love.*

W. Somerset Maugham

"Follow the way of love and eagerly desire spiritual gifts" (1 Cor. 14:1 NIV).

In this statement, the apostle Paul speaks of *the way* of love. However, it isn't straining our purpose here to recognize love as a gift from God to everyone who believes in him. Most certainly, the writer of the First Epistle of John (considered by the earliest Christians and many scholars today to be none other than John the beloved disciple, who also wrote the Gospel of John) seemed to make this point clear when he wrote, "Love is from God; everyone who loves is born of God....God is love" (1 John 4:7–8).

In fact, as we move through the Bible drama from the earliest pages to the end, we have a vivid portrayal of a God who *is* love and who loves. And it was this same Creator-God who shaped human beings in his image who is described by the Gospel writer in these words, "For God so loved the world that he gave his only Son, so that everyone who believes in him may not perish but may have eternal life" (John 3:16). Most assuredly, the gift of love is ours, but the appropriation and expression of that gift is up to us. It is what we do with it that makes the difference.

Sue Monk Kidd is the gifted writer of a delightful book entitled *God's Joyful Surprise*. In it she has some inspired words on God's gift of love: "The joyful experience of being loved by God makes it impossible for us to separate loving God from loving others. No matter how we express our love for one another, we may be sure that God will multiply His presence to us. For we are nearest God when we love."[1]

Unfortunately, because of the plethora of writing on the subject of love, we may fail to catch its full significance due to overfamiliarity. For that reason it is important that we take a second look at a statement John included in his First Epistle, "Love must not be a matter of words or talk; it must be genuine, *and show itself in action* (1 John 3:18 NEB, italics mine). This is a momentous truth; Christian love is not a feeling or an emotion. Rather, it is an act of the will; it is something as John says, *that we do.* It is what we *are*, and it makes a difference in how we act and even how we look.

The apostle Paul is the author of a most beautiful and perceptive poetic essay on the subject of love. When he wrote those paragraphs (preserved for us in the thirteenth chapter of First Corinthians) to his Christian friends in the pagan Greek city of Corinth, he laid himself right on the line. These folks knew the human Paul. He had lived with them, and they had seen him under stress. No, he was not perfect, but, yes, they knew he loved God and he loved them. Paul didn't have to apologize for anything he said in those paragraphs about what it means to love, and I have to believe that his inner feelings of love and his outer actions of love were clearly visible to everyone he met.

In one of his books Frederick Buechner comments that Paul certainly wasn't much to look at, and he quotes a few sentences from the apocryphal *Acts of Paul and Thecla* that were written several years after Paul's death. In this book Paul is described as "baldheaded, bowlegged, strongly built, a man small in size, with meeting eyebrows, with a rather large nose." That is certainly not a particularly flattering physical description, but the payoff comes in the conclusion when the ancient writer adds that "at times he looked like a man, and at times he had the face of an angel."[2] It seems clear that it was Paul's love in action as expressed in his writing and preaching that even made the difference in his appearance as described here.

Paul knew all about the distorted notion of love that was prevalent and that was characteristic of pagan thinking and action in ancient Corinth. He had to have been keenly aware of the temple of Aphrodite that loomed high above the city on the Acrocorinth. It was there that a thousand temple prostitutes entertained in religious orgies, making a mockery of authentic love.

Consequently, it is most significant that Paul, with a magnificent economy of words, lists once and for all his Corinthian Christian friends what it means to act out authentic love:

> *Love is patient; love is kind; love is not envious or boastful or arrogant or rude. It does not insist on its own way; it is not irritable or resentful; it does not rejoice in wrongdoing, but rejoices in the truth. It bears [puts up with] all things, believes all things, hopes all things, endures all things.*
>
> [1 Cor. 13:4–7]

These are all action words—they all speak of something we are or something we do. There is nothing soft and sentimental or licentious in Paul's step-by-step description of love.

At times we might wish that Paul had been a little less specific when he wrote these words. For example, being *patient* and *kind* doesn't come easily for most of us as we make our way through the give-and-take of each twenty-four-hour day. William Barclay commented somewhere in his writings that so much of Christianity is good but unkind. How sad, if true. I suspect it is true, though, as I read and hear about the attacks of some Christians against those who see and interpret their faith differently. Division and disunity are dreadful blights on the teachings of Jesus about love.

By contrast, in writing to the Christians in Colossae Paul gave them and us this powerful love-model, "You are God's chosen people. He loves you and has made you holy. So you must be tender-hearted, kind, humble, gentle, and patient. Bear with one another. If you have reason to complain against someone, forgive him. The Lord forgave you, so you must forgive others. Above all, love one another. *Love makes everything work in perfect harmony*."[3]

At this point, we have to ask, "Where did Paul get this kind of insight? What was his authority for this kind of demanding lifestyle?" After all, before his conversion he had been a rigid and law-abiding Pharisee who was very familiar with the Jewish Creed as spelled out in what he knew as the Shema, the opening words of which are, "Hear, O Israel, the LORD is our God, one LORD, and you must love the LORD your God with all your heart and soul and strength" (Deut. 6:4–5 NEB).

Paul at that time knew that *love* was a dominant theme throughout all of the Book of Deuteronomy. His rigid understanding of that ancient Law, however, obliged him to love only those who interpreted the Law precisely the way he and his fellow Pharisees did. For Paul at that time, his way was the *right* way, and he had been willing to imprison and even kill those who believed differently.

After Paul's conversion to Christ, the way of love took on a deeper and more profound dimension. Undoubtedly, those disciples of Jesus who had been present at the time of his discussion with a certain lawyer had told Paul how Jesus answered the question as to which commandment was the most important. In all probability it was Peter who explained that Jesus had quoted for the lawyer the words from Deuteronomy—words that would have been very familiar to him. Then, in addition, Paul learned that Jesus added a second commandment to the first, "Love your neighbour as yourself" (Mark 12:31 NEB; see also Matt. 22:34–40; Luke 10:25–28).

Paul also would have been told that Jesus followed his recitation of these two commandments with the words, "There is no other commandment greater than these." Wrapped up in these two commandments is the kind of action we are to take with God's gift of love. Here is our model for love of family, of friends, of other Christians, of everybody—every day and always. It is practical, uncomplicated, and straight to the point. We are to love God and express that love in everything we do. We are to love and respect ourselves as people created in the image of God, and we are to love other people with the same degree of intensity that we rightly love ourselves. Peter put it this way, "Above all, keep your love for one another at full strength, because love cancels innumerable sins" (1 Peter 4:8 NEB).

Dr. Eugene Kennedy, the thoughtful and perceptive Christian sociologist and interpreter of love helps us at this point. He writes, "Love always brings us back to the same point of reference. A man must learn to love himself properly if he is to love others at all. This learning is hard because it demands that he sacrifice himself in the process...love takes root as a man becomes increasingly sensitive to others and the effect he has on them....When we are insensitive to ourselves, we can only blunder through life, hurting others even when we do not realize it, leaving the scarred and broken trail that follows always in the wake of rudeness and selfishness."[4]

There is an important thought here that needs to be emphasized. In the past, at least among certain Christians, there has been the tendency to denigrate ourselves in the name of piety, but this sells both God and ourselves short.

In writing to Gentile Christians in Asia Minor, Peter insisted, "You are God's own people. Tell all the world the wonderful things God has done for you....Once you were 'nobody.'...But you have found Christ and now you are 'God's people.' "[5] To be sure, it was God's gift of love that lifted us from being nobody to becoming God's people.

In concluding his marvelous essay on love, Paul summed up all that he had said with these words, "Faith, hope, and love, these three last forever. But the greatest of them all is love."[6] In other words, "Great as faith and hope are, love is still greater. Faith without love is cold, and hope without love is grim. Love is the fire which kindles faith and it is the light which turns hope into certainty."[7]

Throughout our reflections so far on the *gift* and *way* of love no attempt has been made to qualify or explain the use of our English word *love*. The truth of the matter is that for many people today the word *love* is the most abused and confused word in our language. We *love* everything from pizza and our new Buick to the latest soap opera on television.

Tragically, our rather flippant use of the word *love* has stripped it of the passion and intensity that Paul was trying to get across in his Corinthian letter. We are indebted to Professor Elton Trueblood for some helpful thinking on what Paul was actually saying. He suggests that the Greek word Paul used, which translators have rendered *charity* and *love*, has almost no English equivalent. In today's world *charity* refers to forms of philanthropy, and as has already been suggested, so often the word *love* has been over-sentimentalized and trivialized in modern literature and advertising.

Drawing on the suggestion of an English philosopher, Dr. Trueblood endorses the idea that "caring" is "as yet an unspoiled term" and that it is more expressive of Paul's deepest meaning. With this thought in mind, Paul's opening sentence in First Corinthians 13 would read, "If I speak in the tongues of mortals and of angels, but do not care, I am a noisy gong or a clanging cymbal." And verse 8 would open with these words, "Caring never ends."[8]

The meaning of the word *love* as Jesus used it and about which the apostle Paul wrote is passionate and selfless caring. Reflection on this thought throws two vivid pictures onto the screen of my mind. I have written earlier in *Angel Unaware* the story of our little Robin, our Down's syndrome baby. At one point I asked the doctor what Roy and I should do to provide Robin with the best possible care during the time she would be with us.

The doctor's response has been forever etched in my memory, "Take her home and love her. Love will help more than anything else in a situation like this—more than all the hospitals and all the medical science in the world." At that time the doctors were just beginning to talk about the power of tender, loving care as a therapeutic response to illness in the healing process.

The second picture on my mind's screen goes way back to my childhood in central Texas. Christmas was such a joy-filled time in our family as we came together to celebrate the birth of Christ. As children we were, of course, always excited over the exchange of gifts. In looking back now I know that the most precious gift we had was our love for one another. As I wrote in an earlier book, "Is this not the true Christmas? Isn't that what Jesus came to accomplish—'A new commandment I give unto you, That ye love one another....' At least in those first childhood Christmases we began to learn that lesson of love. The gifts were secondary; the greatest gift of all was the plain, simple, gift of love."[9]

NOTES

Chapter 1: **SAY *YES* TO GOD'S GIFT OF TOMORROW**

1. Norman Vincent Peale, "Give Me Tomorrow" (Pawling, N.Y.: Foundation for Christian Living, 1975).

2. Paul Tournier, *The Meaning of Persons* (New York: Harper & Row, 1957), 218.

3. Peale, "Give Me Tomorrow."

4. Frank C. Laubach, *The Inspired Letters* (New York: Thomas Nelson & Sons, 1956), 104, Gal. 6:9–10, italics mine.

5. *Wings of Healing* (San Francisco: Grace Cathedral Ministry of Healing, 1942), 39.

Chapter 2: **SAY *YES* TO GOD'S GIFT OF CHANGE AND GROWTH**

1. Bruce Larson, *The Meaning and Mystery of Being Human* (Waco: Word Books, 1978), 69–70.

2. Michael Marshall, *A Change of Heart* (London: Collins Liturgical Publications, 1981), 18.

3. Marshall, *A Change of Heart*, 20.

4. Paul Tournier, *Learn to Grow Old* (New York: Harper & Row, 1972), 192.

5. Dorothy L. Sayers, *The Mind of the Maker* (Westport, Conn: Greenwood Press, 1971).

6. Evelyn Underhill, *Concerning Inner Life and the House of the Soul* (New York: Methuen, 1947).

7. Ben Campbell Johnson, *The Heart of Paul* (Waco: Word Books, 1976), 92, 2 Cor. 5:16–17, italics mine.

8. Floyd and Harriet Thatcher, *Long Term Marriage* (Waco: Word Books, 1980), 169.

9. Samuel H. Miller, *The Life of the Soul* (New York: Harper & Row, 1951), 17.

Chapter 3: **SAY *YES* TO GOD'S GIFT OF JOY AND LAUGHTER**

1. An excerpt from an old pamphlet originally published by Epworth Press; Elton Trueblood, *The Humor of Christ* (New York: Harper & Row, 1964).

2. Olaf M. Norlie, *The New Testament—A New Translation in Modern English* (Grand Rapids: Zondervan, 1961), Ps. 16:11.

3. James A. Michener, *The World Is My Home* (New York: Random House, 1992), 496.

4. Quoted on the jacket of *I Stand By the Door, the Life of Sam Shoemaker*, Helen Shoemaker (Waco: Word Books, 1967).

5. William Barclay, *The Gospel of Matthew, vol. 1,* rev. ed. (Philadelphia: Westminster Press, 1975), 88.

6. Harold Kushner, *When All You've Ever Wanted Isn't Enough* (New York: Pocket Books, 1986).

7. Fulton J. Sheen, *Treasure in Clay—The Autobiography of Fulton J. Sheen* (Garden City, N.Y.: Doubleday, 1980).

Chapter 4: SAY *YES* TO GOD'S GIFT OF PRAYER

1. Henri J. M. Nouwen, *Reaching Out* (Garden City, N.J.: Doubleday & Company, Inc., 1975), 90.

2. James C. Houston, *The Transforming Friendship* (Oxford: Lion Publishing Co., 1989), 3.

3. William Barclay, *The Gospel of Luke* (Philadelphia: Westminster Press, 1975), 143.

4. Samuel M. Shoemaker, *And Thy Neighbor* (Waco: Word Books, 1967).

5. Norman Vincent Peale, "The World's Greatest Power," PLUS (Pawling, N.Y.: Peale Center for Christian Living, March 1992).

6. Paul S. Rees, *Don't Sleep through the Revolution* (Waco: Word Books, 1969).

Chapter 5: SAY *YES* TO GOD'S GIFT OF WONDER

1. Leslie F. Brandt, *Psalms/Now* (St. Louis: Concordia, 1973), 17, Ps. 8.

2. Brandt, *Psalms/Now*, 17.

3. Carl Sagan, "A Little Blue Dot," *Parade Magazine*, September 9, 1990.

4. Brandt, *Psalms/Now*, 17.

5. Leslie D. Weatherhead, *Key Next Door* (Nashville: Abingdon Press, 1939).

6. Frederick Buechner, *Telling the Truth* (San Francisco: Harper & Row, 1977), 66.

Chapter 6: **SAY *YES* TO GOD'S GIFT OF FRIENDSHIP**

1. Martin E. Marty, *Friendship* (Allen, Tex.: Argus Communications, 1980), 98.

2. Leslie D. Weatherhead, *Key Next Door* (Nashville: Abingdon Press, 1939), 37.

3. M. Scott Peck, *The Road Less Traveled* (New York: Simon & Schuster, 1978).

4. Allen Emory, *Turtle on a Fencepost* (Waco: Word Books, 1979).

Chapter 7: **SAY *YES* TO GOD'S GIFT OF RISK AND DIFFICULTY**

1. Mark O. Hatfield, *Between a Rock and a Hard Place* (Waco: Word Books, 1976), 90–99.

2. C. S. Lewis, *Mere Christianity* (New York: Macmillan, 1943), 171.

3. Paul Tournier, *Learn to Grow Old* (New York: Harper & Row, 1972).

4. Paul Tournier, *The Meaning of Persons* (New York: Harper & Row, 1957), 206.

5. Alan Jones, *Passion for the Pilgrimage* (San Francisco: Harper & Row, 1989), 107.

6. John Knox, *Jesus, Lord and Christ* (New York: Harper & Brothers, 1958), 118.

7. Floyd Thatcher, *The Miracle of Easter* (Waco: Word Books, 1980), 19.

Chapter 8: **SAY *YES* TO GOD'S GIFT OF FAITH**

1. Leslie F. Brandt, *Psalms/Now* (St. Louis: Concordia, 1973), 43.

2. David Jacobsen with Gerald Astor, *Hostage: My Nightmare in Beirut* (New York: Donald I. Fine, 1991), 107.

3. Brandt, *Psalms/Now*, 59.

4. Brandt, *Psalms/Now*, 93.

5. Frank C. Laubach, *The Inspired Letters* (New York: Thomas Nelson & Sons, 1956), 214, 1 John 5:4.

6. C. S. Lewis, *Mere Christianity* (New York: Macmillan, 1943), 69.

7. Pope John Paul II, *The Things of the Spirit*, ed. Kathryn Spink (San Francisco: Harper & Row, 1982), 23–24.

8. Norman Vincent Peale, "Seven Words Can Change Your Life" (Pawling, N.Y.: Foundation for Christian Living, 1976).

Chapter 9: SAY *YES* TO GOD'S GIFT OF HOPE

1. Bruce Larson, *There's a Lot More to Health Than not Being Sick* (Waco: Word Books, 1981), 90.

2. Viktor E. Frankl, *Man's Search for Meaning* (Boston: Beacon Press, 1959), 74–75.

Chapter 10: SAY *YES* TO GOD'S GIFT OF LOVE

1. Sue Monk Kidd, *God's Joyful Surprise* (San Francisco: Harper & Row, 1987), 242.

2. Frederick Buechner, *Peculiar Treasures* (San Francisco: Harper & Row, 1979), 128, 133.

3. Frank C. Laubach, *The Inspired Letters*, Col. 3:12–14, italics mine.

4. Eugene C. Kennedy, *A Time for Love* (Garden City, N.Y.: Doubleday, 1970), 116–117.

5. Laubach, *Inspired Letters*, 1 Pet. 2:9–10.

6. Laubach, *Inspired Letters*, 1 Cor. 13:13.

7. William Barclay, *The Letters to the Corinthians* (Philadelphia: Westminster Press, 1975), 126.

8. Elton Trueblood, *The Yoke of Christ* (New York: Harper & Row, 1958).

9. Dale Evans Rogers, *Christmas Always* (Old Tappan, N.J.: Fleming H. Revell, 1958), 19.

Our Values
Stories and Wisdom

DALE EVANS ROGERS

with Carole C. Carlson

Contents

Preface

Dust filtered into the cluttered office as carpenters shouted instructions over the din of hammers and saws. A major renovation was underway at Roy Rogers' Museum. Dale sat in Roy's brown leather chair, undisturbed by the surrounding confusion. Her son Dusty, business manager of the Rogers' enterprises, and her daughter Cheryl, museum director, stopped briefly to ask her opinion or comment, "Workin' on another book, Mom?" Grandson Dave brought coffee in Styrofoam cups, and great-grandson Dustin came in to get keys and move our cars out of the workmen's path.

Working with Dale is an adventure. Whether we're ducking out of the crowds in an airport, dodging cables and cameras in a television studio, or warming in her memorabilia-filled kitchen, there's a sense of being with a woman who has experienced a lifetime of trials and triumphs.

Dale Evans Rogers belies her eighty-three years. When she walks through a restaurant, heads turn and strangers stop to say, "Hi," as is she were an old friend. (It's mostly those over fifty who recognize her.) Roy and Dale have been known all over the world for their Christian testimony. They have never been reticent to "preach the word ... in season and out of season," no matter what the consequences.

However, today Dale is angry. Not angry-mad, but angry-disturbed.

"What has happened to America's values?" she asked with new seriousness, looking at me across Roy's desk as if I could give her the answers. "Y' know what I mean?" she said in that probing way a mother does when one of the kids needs to repeat what was just said.

So Dale began to define where she stands on the truly important values. The dictionary defines them as "the social principles, goals, or standards held or accepted by an individual, class, or society." *Who or what establishes America's values?* This is the question we must answer, or as Dale says without subtlety, "We will die."

With Dale supplying the core of the ideas and me filling in a little research and providing a few comments, we began this project and discovered in the process that we needed to evaluate our own set of values. The Bible says, "Do not be conformed to this world, but be transformed by the renewing of your mind, that you may prove what is that good and acceptable and perfect will of God" (Rom. 12:2).

Values. We began to tackle the subject in the office of the King of the Cowboys over many cups of lukewarm coffee. Y' know what I mean?

Carole C. Carlson

1

Who Buried America's Values?

Stand fast therefore in the liberty by which
Christ has made us free, and do not be
entangled again with a yoke of bondage.

Galatians 5:1

Since World War II, I have seen this nation slipping from its glory. During that time when we were all working for a common cause, there was a purpose in our unity. I remember going with the radio gang from *The Chase and Sanborn Hour* and entertaining the troops. In those days Edgar Bergen's dummy Charlie McCarthy may have been sassy, but he wasn't dirty. If we had ratings, our shows all would have been G.

Those years were an all-out effort to preserve freedom, and it cost the lives of hundreds of thousands of our young men. When the troops returned and stepped into civilian life, many of them couldn't find jobs because some women refused to step down from the wartime necessity to work, taking pay cuts to keep their jobs. I'm not against women working; I've done it all my life. But in spite of the Ozzie and Harriet image of the 1950s, the place of more and more women working outside the home had become established. Small cracks in the American family were beginning to appear.

When you have lived as long as I have, you have seen many changes. Technology and communication have accelerated like the rising of yeast rolls in a warm oven. I've written most of my books on a yellow lined tablet, scrawled with a pen in airports, lonely hotel rooms, or wherever the spirit moves me. Now my great-grandchildren (thirty of them at this count) have access to computers, CD-ROM, the Internet, and all types of complicated tools that the founders of this Republic would never have dreamed possible.

But have we improved morally and ethically in the same ratio as we have scientifically? Someone has said that man's maximum achievement often falls short of God's minimum demands.

I have witnessed the growing permissiveness in the schools. The front page of a Southern California newspaper recently carried the story of students who went on a hunger strike because they objected to a decision by the board of regents of that school system. The protesters worked a crowd into a jeering frenzy by shouting, "No justice! No peace!" and, "People united will never be divided." But those protests are mild stuff compared to what is happening in many of our schools.

How far have we gone when schools need fences to keep out criminals? When children are gunned down in drive-by shootings? Precious children. I get beside myself seeing such things.

How did the American Dream become so tarnished? Our forefathers came here to escape religious intolerance, but now we see that very intolerance flourishing. God has blessed America bountifully. Will we continue to enjoy that blessing at our present rate of decay?

The Columbus Controversy

In 1992 we experienced the Columbus quincentenary. My goodness, what a flurry that made! It turned out to be more of a controversy than a celebration. Every newsmagazine and the major Protestant and Catholic organizations hotly debated what Columbus's landing really meant. I wondered what all the fuss was about until I realized that the discovery of America was spearheaded by a man who believed God had a destiny for him. Peter Marshall and David Manuel wrote an outstanding book, *The Light and the Glory,* in which they quoted from an obscure volume of Columbus's that had never previously appeared in English. Here is just a short excerpt from that journal:

> *It was the Lord who put into my mind (I could feel His hand upon me) the fact that it would be possible to sail from here to the Indies. All who heard of my project rejected it with laughter, ridiculing me. There is no question that the inspiration was from the Holy Spirit, because He comforted me with rays of marvelous inspiration from the Holy Scriptures.*[1]

Isn't that amazing? I had never heard his faith emphasized. Yet to hear some folks shout "foul" during that five-hundred-year anniversary was enough to think that he was the most devious of men. The National Council of Churches was quoted as issuing this statement:

> *What some historians have termed a "discovery," in reality was an invasion and colonization with legalized occupation, genocide, economic exploitation, and a deep level of institutional racism and moral decadence.*[2]

Excuse me ... now Columbus is branded as a murderer and a racist? Are history books being rewritten?

Legacy of the Pilgrims and Puritans

Calling America a Christian nation today brings cries of protest. We are a country of great diversity, providing opportunity and freedom to people of every nationality and religion, but we must never forget that the values of those first immigrants were based on Christian principles.

I am told that 101 Pilgrims crammed into a space about the size of a volleyball court and spent sixty-six stormy, sickening, stinking days in the inner bowels of a little ship called the *Mayflower*. It's hard to imagine what it would be like confined in such a prison, but I've nursed enough sick children to know that even in the best of circumstances it can be challenging. These folks, however, had a dream to build a life in the New World where they could worship their God in freedom, away from the yoke of the Church of England. Hardships were part of the price.

What must it have been like for those brave folks— undernourished, sick, fearful of what they would encounter in this new land? And then to arrive in November on the East Coast! (I've been a California gal for so long that I get chills opening the refrigerator.)

They believed they were in the Promised Land, even though there were no houses, no roads, and no food. Not exactly a paradise on earth. Before anyone was allowed ashore, all the men signed the Mayflower Compact, promising to submit themselves to the laws enacted by the whole group. Once ashore, William Bradford, a Pilgrim Father, led in a prayer of thanksgiving for delivering them from the perils of the sea and bringing them to America.

All they had to do then was contend with cold, starvation, sickness, and hostile Indians. No problem.

Those Pilgrims were a dedicated group. Living in the desert as I do, it's hard for me to imagine what it would be like in a New England winter, with the men trying to build shelter with hands that were almost frozen, and women trying to feed and warm their children. They soon developed scurvy or died of pneumonia.

In January the roof of the nearly completed common house caught fire, and much of their clothing was burned. By the time spring arrived, they had lost nearly half of their original number. One by one they were buried in the rocky soil.

I know the heartache of losing children. To go on with life is a wrenching experience.

The high point of the week was Sunday worship, when the "beat of a field drum would summon them to the morning and afternoon services."[3]

After that first rugged year, the Pilgrims were blessed with a bountiful harvest from their gardens, and furthermore, in October a crowd of friendly Indians arrived with wild turkeys and other game to celebrate and feast with their new friends. The first Thanksgiving was proclaimed by Governor William Bradford. Here's what Bradford wrote:

> *As one small candle may light a thousand,*
> *so the light kindled here has shown unto many,*
> *yea in some sort to our whole nation ... We have*
> *noted these things so that you might see their worth*
> *and not negligently lose what your fathers have*
> *obtained with so much hardship.*[4]

Today we use little Pilgrim decorations on our Thanksgiving tables and name banks and companies after the *Mayflower,* but we know little of the Pilgrim commitment.

The Puritans were a different breed from the Pilgrims, although both groups were Christians who believed in freedom. The Puritans believed they could live the life to which Christ had called them without separating themselves from the Church of England. They left bawdy, lawless England to establish a Christian community in a new land, thinking they could build the kingdom of God on earth. Those brave men and women made a covenant to live as Christ would have them live in this new land.

A covenant is a commitment to Christ and to one another that we seldom hear about today. It is a *binding* agreement. In rocky New England, God was raising up churches built on stone foundations (Matt. 7:24–27). The Puritans took sin seriously and, consequently, aroused the hatred of Satan. (Lest you wonder if I believe in the reality of Satan, let me emphasize that I do. If Jesus believed in him, then why should I deny his existence?) The Puritans, though, have had bad press in our time. They have been depicted as killjoys who were witch-hunting bigots. To be called "puritanical" is an insult, conjuring up an image of a stiff-necked woman looking down her pince-nez at everyone and everything. The Puritans, for all of their self-righteousness and mistakes, deserve a heap of credit for the direction of our nation.

Backdrop for the Revolution

Before George Washington became the leading man in the great American epic, a few great ministers set New England ablaze with their preaching. Jonathan Edwards, who has been called one of America's greatest Christian thinkers, lit the flame that started what was called the Great Awakening. He preached his most famous sermon, "Sinners in the Hands of an Angry God," in 1741. Now that was a hellfire and brimstone message if there ever was one! (Most modern preachers water that down until it's more like toasted marshmallows.)

Real revival began to sweep through New England, and then along came George Whitefield. He was a fellow whose voice was legendary. His good friend, Benjamin Franklin, once calculated that (in a day before loudspeakers) Whitefield could have been heard by thirty thousand people! Incidentally, Franklin funded a building in Philadelphia for Whitefield to preach in, which later became the University of Pennsylvania.

According to the journal *Christian History,* Whitefield was the most popular figure in America before George Washington.

The first great revival in America where thousands of people accepted Jesus as their Savior brought tremendous spiritual renewal as well as advanced the cause of education. Dartmouth, Princeton, Rutgers, and Brown found their origins in Christian outreach. [5]

Although I cannot call myself an intellectual, I do not believe it is fair to label Christians as anti-intellectuals. Our American roots have been grown in the halls of ivy.

Our Buried History

Carole and I were shocked to read that more than half of America's high school seniors don't know basic facts about U.S. history. In the scores that were released in the month we began this book, November 1995, here were the results: "The history test, given to a national sample of 22,500 fourth, eighth, and twelfth graders found among twelfth graders, only 43 percent attained at least the basic level; 11 percent were proficient; and 1 percent advanced."[6]

Parents, educators, school boards, this is our call for action. It is time to teach the truth of our American roots and instill a pride in our heritage.

2

Value of Our American Heritage

*It cannot be emphasized too strongly
or too often that this great nation was founded,
not by religionists, but by Christians; not on religions,
but on the Gospel of Jesus Christ. For this very reason
peoples of other faiths have been afforded asylum,
prosperity, and freedom of worship here.*

Patrick Henry, 1765

"America was not founded as a Christian nation" is a statement I find hard to swallow. The "Christian Conservative Right" is accused of twisting history to suit its views. On the contrary, I believe the facts contradict that accusation.

Who were the influential men who established our Constitution? What were the basic beliefs of those men and women who founded our great universities, formed our government, and led our nation to greatness? Were they atheists? Buddhists? Muslims? Agnostics?

Our American heritage is under attack by a world-view that is the opposite of that of our Founding Fathers.

Excuse me if I do some flag-waving now. The reputations of some of my heroes are at stake.

George Washington, a Christian

Cherry pies may make us think of George Washington, but the father of our country was a man with deep Christian convictions. Washington's mother was a strong influence on his spiritual life. When he was about twenty, he wrote in a little book some prayers that set the tone for his life. The manuscript was found in the stacks of the Yale Divinity School Library.

We can almost hear him speak in these beautiful prayers.

> **Sunday Morning:** *Let my heart, therefore, gracious God, be so affected with the glory and majesty of Thine honor that I may not do mine own works, but wait on Thee, and discharge those weighty duties which Thou requirest of me ...*

> **Monday Morning:** *Direct my thoughts, words and work, wash away my sins in the immaculate Blood of the Lamb, and purge my heart by Thy Holy Spirit ... daily frame me more and more in the likeness of Thy Son Jesus Christ.*[1]

The legend of the cherry tree and "I cannot tell a lie" may be the only thing a schoolchild will remember about Washington, but his legacy to America is the reminder that our first president was a devout Christian.

History books today may tell of the winter of 1777 when Gen. George Washington and his troops were camped at Valley Forge, where soldiers died at the rate of twelve a day and suffered the freezing cold without blankets or even shoes. The feet and legs of many soldiers turned black with frostbite and had to be amputated. The miracle of Valley Forge is that the men endured at all. The prayers and beliefs of their general sustained them when they could have lost hope. But do the history books tell of Washington's prayers or strong faith?

A pastor of a church near Valley Forge, one of the founders of the Lutheran Church in America, said this about Washington:

> *I heard a fine example today, namely that His Excellency General Washington rode around among his army yesterday and admonished each and every one to fear God, to put away the wickedness that had set in, and to practice the Christian virtues. From all appearances, this gentleman does not belong to the so-called world of society, for he respects God's Word, believes in the atonement through Christ, and bears himself in humility and gentleness. Therefore, the*

Lord God has also singularly, yea marvelously
preserved him from harm in the midst of countless
perils, ambuscades, fatigues, etc., and has hitherto
graciously held him in His hand as a chosen vessel.[2]

When the Revolutionary War was over, the thirteen states were far from being united. In 1787 delegates gathered in Philadelphia for the Constitutional Convention. The quarrels among the states were worse than a large family trying to decide where to have a reunion. The "perfect union" was a perfect mess.

God placed Washington as president of that stormy convention that was to set the course for our country. Historian Page Smith wrote:

His genius was the ability to endure, to maintain his
equilibrium in the midst of endless frustrations, dis-
appointments, setbacks and defeats … George Wash-
ington became the symbol of the American colonists'
determination to endure.[3]

Where do we think Washington got his endurance? Washington himself gives credit to God and prayer. When he was unanimously elected as president of the Constitutional Convention, he said, "Let us raise a standard to which the wise and the honest can repair; the event is in the Hand of God."[4]

The states were arguing over their "sovereign rights" like children over the biggest cookie. Just when it looked as if the debate over representation had deadlocked the entire proceedings, God used an elder statesman, a man who was not an outspoken Christian, to further his plans for our country. Benjamin Franklin, eighty-one-year-old scientist and inventor, said:

> *In the beginning of the contest with Britain, when we were sensible of danger, we had daily prayers in this room for Divine protection. Our prayers, Sir, were heard, and they were graciously answered. All of us who were engaged in the struggle must have observed frequent instances of a superintending Providence in our favor . . . And have we now forgotten this powerful Friend? Or do we imagine we no longer need His assistance?*
>
> *I have lived, Sir, a long time, and the longer I live, the more convincing proofs I see of this truth: "that God governs in the affairs of man." And if a sparrow cannot fall to the ground without His notice, is it probable that an empire can rise without His aid?*
>
> *We have been assured, Sir, in the Sacred Writings that except the Lord build the house, they labor in vain that build it. I firmly believe this.[5]*

The majority of those men who formed the Constitution and the Bill of Rights were Christians. There is no doubt about the beliefs of our first president. Thanks to God, the new nation was getting off to a good start.

Was Lincoln a Christian?

Some people disagree over the beliefs of Abraham Lincoln. Although his profession of faith was not as open as Washington's, his actions point toward a Christian commitment. We came across a copy of a remarkable little book called *Lincoln's Devotional,* which was published in 1852 and inscribed by Lincoln. Agnostics do not usually keep a book of prayer in their possession.

Judge for yourself. Here are a few statements he made:

> *I have been driven many times upon my knees by the overwhelming conviction that I had nowhere else to go. My own wisdom, and that of all about me, seemed insufficient for that day . . .*
>
> *In the very responsible position in which I happen to be placed, being a humble instrument in the hands of our Heavenly Father, as I am, and as we all are, to work out His great purposes, I have desired that all my works and acts may be according to His will, and that it might be so, I have sought His aid.*

His own pastor at the New York Avenue Presbyterian Church said that "the death of Willie Lincoln (his twelve-year-old son) in 1862 and the visit to the Gettysburg battlefield in 1863 finally led Lincoln to personal faith in Christ."[6]

Why debate this issue anymore?

Beliefs of Other American Leaders

In his inaugural address on March 4, 1925, Calvin Coolidge said: "America seeks no empires built on blood and forces … she cherishes no purpose save to merit the favor of Almighty God."

Theodore Roosevelt, the twenty-sixth president of the United States, soldier, author, and Nobel Peace Prize winner, said, "A thorough knowledge of the Bible is worth more than a college education." (I appreciate that statement, since I never went to college.)

In one of his famous fireside chats, President Franklin D. Roosevelt said: "We cannot read the history of our rise and development as a nation, without reckoning with the place the Bible has occupied in shaping the advances of the Republic."

During the darkest days of World War II, and I remember them well, Roosevelt met with British Prime Minister Winston Churchill on a ship in the mid-Atlantic. Roosevelt asked the crew of that American ship to join him in a chorus of "Onward, Christian Soldiers" and described the United States as "the lasting concord between men and nations, *founded on the principles of Christianity*" (emphasis mine!).

Did you know that the "under God" part of the pledge of allegiance was added in 1954 during the Eisenhower administration?

Forty years later, some in America want it eliminated.

A Christian Manifesto

One of our great Christian intellectuals was Francis Schaeffer. When he spoke at the Coral Ridge Presbyterian Church in Florida, he put America's value system in perspective. It wasn't a pleasant picture.

Schaeffer said that Christians are just plain stupid about the lessons of history. "Where have the Bible-believing Christians been in the past forty years?" he asked.

He pointed out that the predominant worldview is humanistic, which places man as the measure of all things. Man must generate values himself, without knowledge from God. This, he said, is the opposite of what the Founding Fathers believed.

Schaeffer warned that when we cut ourselves lose from the law of God, we have a relativistic value system. "We must recognize that this country is almost lost," Schaeffer stated.

As Dale and I (Carole) watched the video of that speech, we wanted to disagree with Francis Schaeffer. America is not lost; it is just wandering. Her people are beginning to wake up and learn the truth about values and ethics again.

We had been involved in some pretty deep thoughts when Dale leaned back in Roy's brown leather chair and asked, "What is truth? Is it really all relative?" She gave me her penetrating look that seemed to expect some definitive answer.

I said, "Let's have lunch."

3

Is Truth Dead?

I have chosen the way of truth;
I have set my heart on your laws.

Psalm 119:30 NIV

A lie is like a twisted ball of yarn. When you try to find the end, you only get more entangled. Early in my acting career, I became involved in a deception that I rationalized because of personal ambition. My career was more important than my honesty.

It all began when I was a rebellious high school kid and eloped with a handsome boy, both of us lying about our ages to get a marriage license. The marriage was a terrible failure, but I was blessed with a wonderful son, Tom. My faithful mother helped me raise him, or I would have been destitute.

As Tom began to grow, I was determined to provide an education and a good life for him. I took him to church, believing that he needed to know the Lord and live by his principles. As for me, I had begun to sing with dance bands, on radio, and in fancy hotels. I believed that Jesus might make demands on me that would interfere with my career, so I avoided making a commitment to him. My integrity was blinded by ambition.

The test really came when I was summoned to Hollywood for a screen test. My son was twelve years old and I was twenty-eight. Being that age and having a son that old were unacceptable for a leading lady in the movie industry of the 1940s. The solution was for me to say that I was twenty-one and that Tom was my brother. I agreed to that bold-faced lie in order to get a contract with Twentieth Century-Fox.

As my career progressed, my guilt grew. Tom became a dedicated young Christian, and one day he told me he couldn't lie as I was lying, even for me. That hurt. But I was too far into the mud to be able to climb out.

Years later, God convicted me of my deceit. That story is told in the next chapter. However, I can understand how the desires of the heart, if not guided by God's principles, can squeeze you into the world's mold. Lying can become such a habit that even the liar does not know what the truth is.

Truth: Endangered Species

Several years ago, Allan Bloom, a professor at the University of Chicago, made some startling observations. He shook the academic community with his statements about modern education. He said:

> *There is one thing a professor can be absolutely certain of: almost every student entering the university believes, or says he believes, that truth is relative . . . Relativism is necessary to openness; and this is the virtue, the only virtue, which all primary education for more than fifty years has dedicated itself to inculcating. Openness—and the relativism that makes it the only plausible stance in the face of various claims to truth and various ways of life and kinds of human beings—is the great insight of our times. The true believer is the real danger . . . The point is not to correct the mistakes and really be right; rather it is not to think you are right at all.*[1]

If Bloom was correct, and I believe he was, then our educational system is spawning young men and women who have no conception of right and wrong. If truth is relative, then what or who are they to believe? Their parents? The most popular professor? Current political thought?

Someone said that labels should be on jars of jam, not people, but today we label people for identification. "Baby Busters" is a label applied to those people born between 1965 and 1983. George Barna, who heads a research group that makes statistics interesting, said in his book *Baby Busters: The Disillusioned Generation,* that "to the typical Buster, there is no such thing as absolute truth. Statistically, 70% claim that all truth is relative and personal."[2]

These kids are saying that nothing can be known for certain except the things they experience in their own lives. They have been told, "Do what comes naturally. If it feels good ... do it."

Is it any wonder that we are facing a moral crisis in America? A free society cannot survive with people who habitually lie, cheat, and have no standards of truth. When children want to accuse someone of fibbing, they point their fingers and chant, "Liar, liar, pants on fire." We should be burning with shame for becoming people who cannot be trusted.

I can remember when a man's handshake was his word. Today we sign contracts in triplicate.

Time magazine had a story a few years ago with one of the ugliest pictures on the cover that I've ever seen. It was a close-up of a grinning face leering at you with a diabolical smile. The title was, "Lying ... everybody's doin' it (honest)." The article was an indictment against politicians. "The public may now assume lying on the part of its representatives because it expects them to lie."[3]

For government to be effective, we need some degree of honesty. I don't look at what our representatives say; I examine who they are. What are their bedrock beliefs? Do they just mouth a belief in God, or do they live it?

The Busters are not the only disillusioned ones. In a magazine for senior citizens (about forty million of us), it was said, "America is headed straight to hell, figuratively and literally, unless it changes course soon."[4]

Listen to the statistics from the senior category (who should know better!). Answering the question, "What's the best way to halt declining values?" the largest number, 35 percent, answered, "Shore up governmental and personal responsibility." Yet how can moral decline be halted if neither government nor individuals have a standard for truth?

The Book of Truth

One of our most popular presidents was Dwight Eisenhower, who was commander of Allied forces in Europe during World War II and president of the United States from 1953 to 1961.

Roy and I, along with the Riders of the Purple Sage, were invited to Washington to entertain for David Eisenhower's birthday. I'll never forget a conversation I had with Mamie Eisenhower. She said, "We still sleep in the same bed, and sometimes at night I wake up and find him gone. He's usually in the garden, pacing back and forth and praying for guidance."

I guess I knew that Ike was a Christian but I never realized the depth of his belief. He was a president who built his life on the words of the Bible to a greater degree than most people know. He said,

> *The Bible is endorsed by the ages. Our civilization is built upon its words. Like stored wisdom, the lessons of the Bible are useless unless they are lifted out and employed. A faithful reading of Scripture provides the courage and strength required for the living of our time.*[5]

It doesn't do any good to have millions of Bibles on bookshelves unless the truths within their pages are applied to our lives. It doesn't do any good for a witness to place his hand on the Bible and swear to tell "the whole truth, nothing but the truth, so help me God" unless the Bible is the basis of that person's belief system. He might as well swear on a comic book!

Jesus said, "I am the way, the truth, and the life. No one comes to the Father except through me" (John 14:6). When you think of it, probably no other words ever said have been more disputed than those. There is only one way to God and that is through faith in Jesus Christ. And that is the truth.

Verily, Verily

In the King James Version of the Bible, we read over and over that Jesus said, "Verily, verily," which in the newer translations is "I tell you the truth ... I tell you the truth." If Jesus did not tell us the truth, millions of people throughout history have been living the big lie. If Jesus did not tell us the truth, my life has been based on a fraud.

Jesus had been arrested in the Garden of Gethsemane, bound, beaten, and dragged to Pilate's court. Imagine the scene. Jesus, charged with rebellion, stood before the Roman governor of Judea and was asked, "Are you the king of the Jews?" (John 18:33 NIV).

Jesus did not look like a king; he did not live like a king; so the men who guarded him jeered and mocked. Jesus answered: "You are right in saying I am a king. In fact, for this reason I was born, and for this I came into the world, to testify to the truth. Everyone on the side of truth listens to me" (John 18:37 NIV).

Pilate answered with that universal question, "What is truth?" (John 18:38 NIV).

Why didn't Pilate understand that Jesus had just told him that he was truth? Sometimes when faced with such clear and simple statements, a person can't understand. When I hear some of the complicated gobbledygook that people use to rationalize the truth of God, I think if they had actually been present at the trial of the ages, they would have sided with Pilate.

Jesus has told us over and over again in the Bible that he was telling us the truth. Here are just a few examples:

> *I tell you the truth, anyone who will not receive*
> *the kingdom of God like a little child will*
> *never enter it. (Luke 18:17 NIV)*
> *In reply Jesus declared, "I tell you the truth,*
> *no one can see the kingdom of God unless*
> *he is born again." (John 3:3 NIV)*
> *I tell you the truth, he who believes has everlasting*
> *life. (John 6:47 NIV)*

The Bible also warns us that not everyone will rush to put out a welcome mat for the truth:

> *Even from your own number men will arise and dis-*
> *tort the truth in order to draw away disciples*
> *after them. (Acts 20:30 NIV)*
> *Many will follow their shameful ways*
> *and will bring the way of truth into disrepute.*
> *(2 Peter 2:2 NIV)*
> *They exchanged the truth of God for a lie, and wor-*
> *shiped and served created things rather than*
> *the Creator—who is forever praised. Amen.*
> *(Rom. 1:25)*

Many are trying to kill truth today, but the Bible says that if we take the sword of the Spirit, which is the Word of God, we can extinguish all the flaming arrows of the evil one (see Eph. 6:13–18).

Truth is not dead. It can be found in the Bible I hold in my hand right now. Truth is alive for now and eternity.

4

My Search for Life's Values

I love the LORD,
because He has heard my voice.
Psalm 116:1

My story has been told in more detail in *The Woman at the Well*, but a capsule version of it is needed here to give the background on how my life was one continual search for solid values.

I was born Frances Octavia Smith and was a real handful growing up. I didn't live up to the dignity of my name. As the spoiled first grandchild, I wanted to be the center of attention and did my best to stay there.

One of my earliest memories is going to a little Baptist church in Italy, Texas, where my mother played the piano. I loved music and sometimes when a hand-clapping gospel song began, I would scoot out of our pew and dance in the aisle. That just wasn't done in a Baptist church.

A switch was frequently applied to my backside; but my psyche was never injured, just my pride. I shudder to think of what I might have been if no one cared enough to discipline me.

Granddaddy Wood was a great influence in my life. He never lost his zest for living or his love for children. When I was very small, he said something about me that was almost prophetic. "She'll die hard, with her head up!" Many times I've recalled those words of Grandpa's. When life has dealt me tough blows, I've been given the strength to handle them and come back bruised but not broken.

I was blessed with a Christian upbringing, although I shoved it in the background in later years. This should give hope to parents of prodigal sons or daughters. Teach the little ones now; grasp the few years of their childhood and point them toward Jesus. Solomon said, "Remember now your Creator in the days of your youth, before the difficult days come" (Eccles. 12:1).

Both my father and mother went to Christian colleges and instilled in me the importance of education. They taught me how to read and do simple arithmetic before I entered school, so I skipped half of the first grade, all of the second, and went right into the third grade. I don't believe that was wise, because children miss too many valuable experiences when they are forced to grow up fast. But I loved school and I also loved music. I started taking piano lessons but I soon became impatient with those endless exercises and began to improvise. My poor piano teacher told my parents that I was wasting her time and their money. She gave up on me. I played by ear from then on and music has been a part of my life and career. It must have been a part of God's plan that I never turned into a whiz at the piano.

Sundays we went to Sunday school, church, and an evangelistic service at 7:30 in the evening. I was expected to be there, and it never dawned on me to goof off and not go until I reached my early teens. When parents ask me today, "Should I make my children go to church?" I usually ask them if they go to church. If they say yes, then I'm free to say, "Don't you think your children should go where you're going?" If they say no, I ask, "Then why should you expect your children to go?"

I don't want to give the impression that churchgoing makes a person a Christian. I remember Corrie ten Boom saying, "A mouse in a cookie jar isn't a cookie!" On the other hand, I do believe that Christians who think they can worship without church attendance are only fooling themselves. The Bible says, "Let us not neglect our church meetings, as some people do, but encourage and warn each other, especially now that the day of his coming back again is drawing near" (Heb. 10:25 LB).

When I was a kid, church and school were partners in

training children. In school we began each day with a short prayer and had chapel every Friday morning, with different ministers giving a devotional. Even those kids who didn't go to church got a dose of Bible teaching. I don't know of anyone suing the school board for allowing such outrageous teaching! I believe it is a tragic mistake that separation of church and state has been so misinterpreted that God is left out of the classroom.

When I was ten, our church had an old-time revival meeting with an itinerant evangelist. He talked a lot about hell, and I decided it wasn't a place I wanted to go. I walked down the aisle and received Jesus Christ as my Savior. However, for many years I refused to surrender my life wholeheartedly to him.

I wanted to run things my way, thank you.

My mother used to say I was "born grown." It was that attitude that caused the first serious problem in my life.

Too Young to Marry

When kids go astray, parents often blame themselves. "What did we do wrong?" they moan. My parents may have made mistakes, but it wasn't their fault that I became rebellious. I was only fourteen when I started going with a handsome boy who was a few years older than me. When our relationship looked like it was getting out of hand, I was forbidden to see him. Defying my parents' wishes, I met him secretly. One day we decided to elope. Lying about our ages, we obtained a marriage license and were wed in the home of a minister.

I shall never forget the agonizing silence on the other end of the phone when I called my mother to tell her we were married. When she finally spoke, it was to ask us to come home. We went home the next day.

Mother pleaded with me to go back to high school since I had another year before graduation. Still in defiance of authority, I refused.

Tom was born, and when he was six months old, his father announced that he was too young to be tied down. I was only sixteen and already facing divorce.

The Critical Decade

Dr. James Dobson calls the years between sixteen and twenty-six "the critical decade." I think every decade is critical, but that period was a time of searching for my purpose in life. Trying to deal with the pain of a ruined marriage and support a child, I struggled to find my way.

Church became important to me again, and I began to read my Bible. I was told I needed to learn a skill; so I went to business school, although my heart was in show business. While working as a secretary, I even tried writing short stories. After the rejection slips piled up, I was convinced I would never get anything published.

After work I spent most of my time singing and accompanying myself on the piano. One day the big chance came to be a guest on a radio program. It was the foot in the door I needed. From radio, I began to get opportunities to sing with dance bands. Then I decided that if I could crack the market in small towns, I could win in the Windy City. So I took Tommy and went to Chicago. A few struggling years later, however, I lost the fight. Sick and broke, I wired my folks for money and went home to Texas.

My precious mother cared for Tommy while I regained my strength. He called her Mom and me Sassie. (Frances was too hard to pronounce.) She was more of a mother to him in those early years than I was. I was more like a big sister.

My ambition drove me and dominated my life. One time Tommy was very sick during a polio epidemic. I was frantic with fear as he was taken to the hospital for a spinal tap. I promised God that I would put him first in my life if my son's test was negative. It was.

For a few weeks I prayed and read my Bible every day. But once again, my relationship with God took a backseat to my musical ambition.

Overnight success is the stuff movies and fairy tales are made of. One value I learned early on was to work hard. I was on the staff of a Louisville, Kentucky, station when I met a pianist-arranger who became my husband.

It looked like that rainbow was within reach. We went to Chicago, and this time I began to sing at the fancy hotel ballrooms. Frances Smith was transformed into Dale Evans. Show business became my life.

Sure, I took Tom to church because I wanted him to have a solid relationship with the Lord; but as for me, I held back from an all-out commitment, afraid that the Lord might demand something from me that I was not willing to give. He might even ask me to give up my career, and I wasn't willing to do that.

Hollywood, though, was not my goal. I wanted to do musical comedy in New York. Besides, I didn't think I was pretty enough for the movies, and I certainly did not consider myself an actress. One day, however, I got a telegram from an agent in California. This was heady stuff. Without going into all the steps that led me to the glitter capital of the world, let me just say that this was a time when my values were not as important as the tinsel in the studios. This was when I lied about my age and tried to pass off Tom as my brother.

Something was very wrong with my life. No amount of busyness filled the emptiness I felt. I went to church with Tom and my husband, but between Sundays I read books on peace of mind, Eastern philosophy, and even mysticism.

World War II was in full swing, and I did a lot of shows for the boys in the service. Because we were so busy, my husband and I were seeing less and less of each other. I was making four hundred dollars a week and working like a Texas ranch hand. While America was unified in the war effort, my husband and I were drifting further apart.

With my "critical decade closing, I lived with a sense of failure and an emptiness of spirit.

Riding the Career Bronco

By the time I met Roy Rogers, I had encountered enough Hollywood types to know the difference between the real thing and a phony. Roy was genuine. When I landed a contract to play opposite him in a film, I neglected to tell anyone that I couldn't ride a horse. The first day on location I was put to the test. There was a horse that looked as big as a barn to me, and I didn't even know which side to get on. Roy just looked at me with that crinkly-eyed smile of his and said, "I thought you could ride."

Believe me, after several near disasters, I did learn to ride.

Roy was a straight-shooter in every way. In the studio, we were a family: Roy, Gabby Hayes, Pat Brady, the Sons of the Pioneers, and me. We made more than thirty films and knew the best and the worst of each other. The worst of me was my growing ego.

The drive for personal success is a factor that unbalances any life. My ambition was like a runaway stallion. I didn't realize it then but I was sacrificing the most precious things in life to satisfy my personal desires.

In 1945 my husband and I were divorced. I was more devoted to the demands of the Hollywood system than to our marriage. We had working hours that kept us apart. I was a day person, and he was a musician and a night person.

Meanwhile, "back at the ranch," my son Tom was being nurtured through those crucial teen years by my mother. He had developed into a fine Christian, no thanks to me. Oh sure, I had declared my faith in God and in Jesus Christ, but it was on the back burner, and the fire wasn't on.

God's Mysterious Ways

Roy was married to Arline, a very pretty girl, and they had two children: Cheryl, an adopted daughter who was a Shirley Temple look-alike, and Linda Lou, a quiet child with sparkling eyes. Roy was proud of his girls. Church and Sunday school, though, were not a part of their life. Roy had told us during gab sessions on the set that he could not reconcile a loving God with the suffering he saw when he visited children's hospitals all over the country. He had questions I could not answer.

Arline gave birth to Roy Jr., by cesarean section, but she died eight days later because of a blood clot following surgery. Roy was devastated.

After Arline's death, Roy struggled to find help to run

his home and care for his children. He worked unbeliev-
ably long hours and made personal appearance tours to
make the money he needed to support his family.

As time went on, we realized that our relationship was
deepening beyond our movie partnership. However, neither of us wanted to rush into marriage.

I must say, I probably had one of the most unromantic
proposals in the book. We were sitting on our horses in
the chutes during a rodeo in the Chicago Stadium. It was
in the fall of 1947. Roy leaned over his saddle and said,
"What are you doing New Year's Eve?" That seemed rather
strange to me, since New Year's Eve was months away.

We were waiting to be introduced and have the gates
opened for us to gallop out before the crowd. I said, "No
plans."

He said, "Well, why don't we get married?"

I said, "Yes!" and just then the announcer shouted,
"And now, the King of the Cowboys and the Queen of the
West ... Roy Rogers and Dale Evans!"

In 1947 I understood very little of God's mysterious
ways.

House Built on Rock

When we were married on New Year's Eve, we thought
we were keeping it a secret. The intrepid Louella Parsons,
though, who seemed to know everything about everybody

in Tinseltown, broke the news on radio and also broadcast that I had a grown son. Frankly, Tom and I were relieved that the long deception I had played was over.

As Roy and I began to build our life together, we faced many challenges. First of all, I was a stepmother. I hadn't considered myself a very good mother to my own Tom, but now there were three more. My career had to take a backseat with the new responsibilities. It was all so overwhelming.

Tom was a teenager but with wisdom beyond his years. He suggested that God could help me do what I felt inadequate to do. And he thought I should take the children to church. The next Sunday I went to an evening service with him.

The preacher gave a sermon on "The House That Is Built on the Rock." He said that any house built on the rock of faith in Jesus Christ would stand up against anything that life could throw at you. I thought about my ego, my lies, all my failures, and it seemed like my very soul was shouting, "You are guilty, Dale Evans Rogers. You are a sinner."

Until that time, I thought a sinner was the drunk who staggered down Main Street or the producer who demanded the starlet to sleep with him. Then I realized that Scripture says, *"All* have sinned and fall short of the glory of God" (Rom. 3:23, emphasis added).

Even though I had walked the aisle many years before,

the following Sunday I bounced out of my pew and rushed forward. This time when I gave my life to Christ, it was more than lip service. I asked him to forgive me and accept me just as I was. *This time* I asked him to create in me a right spirit, to break me if he had to. I surrendered my life to use for his glory.

How can I describe the peace that came over me? The emptiness in my life was gone; in its place was a joy that surpassed anything I had ever experienced. Now when I sang "How Great Thou Art," I knew the meaning of the words.

Roy was less than thrilled when I burst into the house and said, "Honey, I've just made the greatest decision of my life; I've dedicated my heart and life to Jesus Christ!"

Roy was glad to see me so enthusiastic but he must have chosen his words carefully, for he said, "Mama, if it makes you happy, fine. But please don't go overboard and don't go to work on me."

He said those words in a spirit of love, and I accepted them that way. I loved him too much to force him into his own decision.

I began taking the children to Sunday school and church, reading the Bible at dinner, and hearing their prayers. Roy started to notice a change in me, although he didn't say anything. One Sunday, after a rip-roarin' Saturday night argument following a party at our house, Roy announced that he was going to church with us.

When the sermon was over, as was the custom in that church, an invitation to accept Christ was given. Roy sat straight up (he had his eyes closed during the sermon, and I thought he was dozing) and said, "Mama, I'm going down there."

Roy made his own decision, without any prodding from me, and I was never happier in my life. Now our house was truly being built on a Rock. Gradually God began to break this ego and pride of mine and show me his values for my life.

5

Value of
Tough Times

We are hard pressed on every side,
yet not crushed;
we are perplexed, but not in despair;
persecuted, but not forsaken;
struck down, but not destroyed.

2 Corinthians 4:8–9

*T*he Bible has red lights. Sometimes I've breezed through the warning signs without stopping. One that slowed me down, however, was raised by an old fisherman named Peter. He said, "Do not think it strange concerning the fiery trial which is to try you, as though some strange thing happened to you" (1 Peter 4:12).

The best way to survive those fiery trials is by holding the hand of the Lord. When the three Hebrew youths were thrown into the furnace by order of Nebuchadnezzar, they walked out unscathed. Walking with them was their fourth companion—Jesus. Without him, they would have been a heap of charred bones.

Are we Christians prepared to be persecuted for our faith? Have we prepared ourselves for tough times?

The Bible says, "All who desire to live godly in Christ Jesus will suffer persecution" (2 Tim. 3:12). And Jesus warned that as the time of his return comes closer, "They will lay their hands on you and persecute you" (Luke 21:12).

Now I'm not saying we should all get persecution complexes when tough times hit. Compared to Christians in many parts of the world, we Christians in America have had it pretty easy. However, in subtle ways we're beginning to see the foreshadowing of persecution happening now.

It's one thing to be labeled with derision as the "Christian Right," but it's another to be tortured for our faith.

Billy Graham asked the probing question:

> Are we too soft, too used to the luxuries of freedom,
> that we would be unable to stand up to persecution?
> Most of us would do no more, no less, than we are
> doing right now. Some of us who wear our Christianity
> on our sleeves would probably be the first to surrender.
> Many would be modern-day Peters who would say,
> "Though all others deny Christ, yet I will never deny
> him." But he did. Three times.[1]

When you go into a jewelry store to look for a particular ring or necklace, the master jeweler will place a black velvet cloth on the counter so that the stone or chain will look its best. It has been said that we are God's jewels, and often he exhibits his gems on a dark background so they will shine more brightly too.

Some of us, though, need more polishing than others to show our value.

Tough times are as inevitable in life as ants at a picnic. None of us wants them; all of us will have them. Tough times come in many forms ... the death of a loved one, sickness, financial woes, broken relationships. The good news is that we can be prepared, because God gives us the tools in his book to equip us.

Why Me?

The "Why me?" complex is common among the afflicted. I guess the correct answer would be, "Why not?" If life was all "Happy Trails," then we'd never know how to ride through the bristles and swamplands and deserts.

Lieutenant Clebe McClary lost one arm and an eye in a fierce grenade attack in Vietnam. This young man, a handsome, disciplined athlete, came home from the war with a shattered body and what he thought was a shattered life. Clebe wrote in his book, *Living Proof,* "I don't think my suffering was in vain. The Lord has used my experiences for good by drawing many lives to Him. It's hard to see any good that came from the war in Vietnam, but I don't believe our effort was wasted. Surely some seed was planted for Christ that cannot be stamped out."[2]

Barbara Johnson is a person who has taken life's blows and turned them into humor. In a world of so much tragedy, she is able to lighten the load with her own sense of compassionate joy. One chapter title in her book *Splashes of Joy in the Cesspools of Life* was "Laugh and the World Laughs with You ... Cry and You Simply Get Wet."

From the tragedies in her life, Barbara has touched the lives of many who have forgotten how to laugh. Her ministry could be based on Solomon's words: "To everything there is a season ... a time to weep, and a time to laugh" (Eccles. 3:1, 4).

Life gives us bumps, but laughter is a shock absorber that eases the blows.

Many know the story of Joni Eareckson Tada, the beautiful woman who is a quadriplegic, permanently confined to a wheelchair. Joni paints by holding a brush with her teeth, writes with brilliance, and sings with joy in her heart. I have appeared on programs with her, and her testimony about the value of tough times touches us all.

Tim Hansel was an experienced mountain climber, but in one terrifying fall down a glacier, he was doomed to a lifetime of constant pain. He wrote in his book *You Gotta Keep Dancin'*, "I can't remember when I last woke up feeling good. Each morning continues another layer of nauseating pain, stiffness, the dull gray ache, and the never-ending fatigue. It's been a little over ten years since my accident. Life was different before then; I just can't remember what it felt like."[3]

Yet Hansel learned how to have joy in the midst of pain. One line in his diary said, "He who laughs ... lasts."

Roy and I have tried to be ambassadors of joy to children around the world, but God used some of our own children to teach us the value of tears and tough times.

His Angels' Charge over Me

When God chose to give us little Robin Elizabeth, after doctors had told me I could not have another child, I knew before I left the hospital that there was something severely wrong with our little miracle baby. They told me she was mongoloid, and perhaps it would be better if we institutionalized her from the beginning.

Robin had been dedicated to the Lord, and in spite of our heartbreak, I felt that she would be used to glorify him in some way.

God took Robin home to be with him when she was two years old. Her story in the little book *Angel Unaware* went around the world. For the two years she was with us, she taught me some lasting lessons on true values in life.

What could a child with a severe disability teach us? She taught us that the strength of the Lord is made perfect through weakness. She taught us humility, patience, gratitude, and dependence on God.

As I look back more than forty-four years to the short time we had with Robin, I remember it was a period filled with heavy sadness and joyous excitement. After she died, I was driven (I think that's more accurate than "inspired") to write *Angel Unaware*.

People have asked me about the title of the book. It comes from Hebrews 13:1 (KJV): "Be not forgetful to entertain strangers; for thereby some have entertained angels unawares."

Only God himself could have taken that little book and turned it into a best-seller. Hundreds of thousands of people with exceptional children were able to find new confidence because God had spoken to them through Robin and through us.

Two months after Robin's death, we adopted a bright little Choctaw Indian baby we named Dodie; and shortly afterwards, Sandy, a five-year-old boy with physical and psychological problems, became a part of the family. In 1954 we took a foster child, Marion Fleming, from a church orphanage in Edinburgh, Scotland.

I believe Roy's heart was big enough to hold all the children of the world, and I just rode alongside him.

The Growing Years

When Dodie was three and a half, God brought us another blessing in the arms of Dr. Bob Pierce, the founder of World Vision. Little In Lee was a Korean orphan whom we named Debbie Lee, a child full of bubbling joy. Now we had Cheryl and Linda Lou, Dusty (Roy Jr.), Dodie, Sandy, Marion, and Debbie. Our hands were now full with seven young children, one grown son, two careers, and a challenge a minute.

We raised our blended family with discipline combined with unconditional love. But we had definite rules of behavior for the Rogers' clan.

Dusty and Sandy were a handful. They could be twin terrors. When I took them shopping, they sat in the backseat of the car. I carried a switch to referee their wrestling matches. Once I applied a swift sting of discipline to Dusty's derriere.

"Mom, I'm leaving home!" he howled. "Good idea," I said. "We'll pack your suitcase as soon as we get home." It was very quiet for a few minutes. "Well, maybe I'll wait a year or two," he mumbled under his breath.

Naughty or nice, I think children are terrific. Jesus certainly set the example for us when he told his disciples to bring the children to him. I have sung, "Jesus loves the little children, all the children of the world. Red and yellow, black and white, they are precious in His sight," so many times that when I see an adult neglecting, abusing, or spoiling a precious child, I am filled with revulsion and cannot find the words to describe my anger.

As the children grew, so did our faith. We became a part of the Hollywood Christian group, people who were prominent in the industry and bold enough to stand for Christ in a largely anti-Christian atmosphere. We had a meeting every Monday night in different homes. Billy Graham came to one of the first meetings in our backyard around the swimming pool. It was the beginning of a relationship that has spanned the years.

Roy says, "Every time Billy walks into a room the lights come on." We can testify to the fact that we are among the millions whose lives have been touched by this great man.

In the summer of 1963, Billy came to the Los Angeles Memorial Coliseum for a major crusade. This was a milestone for the Rogers family, for on Youth Night, Dusty, Sandy, Dodie, and Debbie went down the aisle onto that immense field and gave their hearts to Jesus. My cup was running over.

At the same crusade in 1963, my coauthor, Carole, said that her entire family accepted the Lord.

All of this is just a brief background to more of those tough times. How quickly our joy turned to sorrow. A year after Debbie dedicated her life to Christ, she met him face-to-face. In 1964 our precious twelve-year-old was killed in a church bus accident. I didn't think I could stand losing another child.

Roy was in the hospital after an operation, and his surgeon told him the wrenching news of Debbie's death. Because of Roy's hospitalization, we could not lean on each other's strength at this time. I don't know how people get through times like this without the Lord.

Soon after her funeral, I was guided (yes, that can happen) to write the book *Dearest Debbie* to help those mothers and fathers who might lose their Debbies.

And Then There Was Sandy

In 1965 our Sandy enlisted in the army. He had been a battered child and had physical and psychological injuries that never completely healed; but he wanted to prove himself worthy as a man, and the one way he knew how was to join the army. When we saw him off for basic training, I had a premonition that we might never see him again.

Sandy did come home once more, to become officially engaged. Then he was sent to Germany and, through a tragic accident, died in an army camp there. Some of his buddies dared him to chugalug to prove that he was man enough to wear his first-class stripes. He was killed by an overdose of alcohol during that "I dare you" drinking session.

In one of his letters to us, Sandy had written, "Put your faith in the Lord because He's always around when you need Him. All He asks in return is your heart and devotion."

No Pity Party

Roy and I have had our share of hospital stays in the last few years, but we're not inviting any of you to a pity party. I've discovered that you can always find someone whose troubles are worse than your own.

Tough times? Child stuff compared to what the person who has rejected Christ will experience during the Great Tribulation. I would not want anyone to go through those days. That is the reason I will speak and write until the Lord says, "You've stayed down there long enough, Dale; it's time to come home."

Right now he says to us in his Book: "For our light affliction, which is but for a moment, is working for us a far more exceeding and eternal weight of glory" (2 Cor. 4:17).

Yes, partners, that's good news.

6

Family Values in a Fractured World

As for me and my house,
we will serve the LORD.
Joshua 24:15

What is a "dysfunctional" family? When we were raising our blended family of different nationalities, we had never heard of the term. Look it up—it means abnormal, impaired, incomplete. Is that the norm in America today?

Dan Quayle struck a raw spot in the American psyche when he started the commotion about family values. Though he stirred up a lot of controversy—just because he spoke the truth about immorality in the entertainment industry—what he had to say was worth hearing. Quayle said, "Despite their differences, families are united by such qualities as responsibility, communication, love and respect, faith and community involvement."[1]

Right on, Dan! The American family may be under attack, but it's not dead.

Family Foes

Roy says, "When the enemies of our freedom under God are successful in breaking up our homes, they have broken our backs—because the home is the backbone of America."

Our backbone is being weakened today by a befuddled society that looks in the wrong places for family values.

Remember when the family hour on television was for families? Broadcasters used to set aside the 8 to 9 P.M. hour as a safe time for children to watch television. *The Brady Bunch,* the wholesome teenagers in *Happy Days,* and *The Cosby Show* were entertainment havens for big and little couch potatoes. However, even the traditional family viewing hour on Sunday nights is now filled with explicit sexual references, off-color language, and violence. I doubt that the stories Roy and I did, where the good guys won over the bad guys, would pass a network's proposal stage. Too goody-two-shoes for today's viewers.

An article in the *Los Angeles Times* stated: "The networks have narrowed their target viewing audience to adults, primarily between the ages of 18 and 49, because advertisers believe they are the key consumers in America."[2]

When it comes to money versus morals, we know what wins.

The Kaiser Foundation funded a report on "Sex and the Mass Media" and concluded that the media's "love affair with sex and romance" contributes to irresponsible sexual behavior among young people, including unplanned and unwanted pregnancies.[3]

Talk shows are so frank that nothing is sacred. It astounds me that people will divulge their sins so openly. Dirty linen should be thrown in the washing machine, not hung out on the lamppost for everyone to see!

What about language? We have become so desensitized to raw and profane words that they don't have an impact anymore. A friend of mine had her office next to a school playground, and she said that the words that came out of the children sounded like those of hardened street thugs.

Network executives claim that they are just reacting to the needs of the marketplace. What is watched sells advertising, they rationalize. Look, the television moguls say, it's the parents who must take responsibility for what their children see. I agree with that, but somehow it doesn't cut to the core of the problem. When good taste and moral values are abdicated, it's everybody's responsibility to change things. Don't the media makers have children too?

The triune god of today is money, sex, and power.

Before Cradle and Grave

What is human life worth? Millions of babies are killed every day by abortions. One of the foremost debates in America is over the rights of a woman to choose to abort and the rights of a child to live. The Bible says: "your eyes saw my substance, being yet unformed. And in Your book they all were written, The days fashioned for me, When as yet there were none of them" (Ps. 139:16). God knew us in our mother's womb: "Before I formed you in the womb I knew you" (Jer. 1:5). Abortion is one of the greatest crimes in America and should be called what it is ... murder.

The unborn child has no rights, and the elderly are burdens. We do not want to be saddled with aged parents, so they are farmed out to nursing homes. Many parents also dread being "a burden to their children." What about the burdens we were to them in our childhood? What about the nights our parents lost sleep because of our ailments and fretfulness? Our elderly should be viewed as blessings, not burdens.

Where is the dignity of maturity? Why are we so loathe to age? Why do we spend thousands of dollars on face-lifts, tummy tucks, chin tucks, buttock lifts, and breast implants to try to escape the aging process? As I told a columnist for the *Los Angeles Times* who accused me of having a face-lift, "No, I have not had a face-lift. What's the point? I could lift everything in my body, but inside is the same old mileage."

Every stage of our life is important ... and, I might add, rewarding.

The New American Family

A typical family is as obsolete as the Edsel. Gone are the days when June Cleaver was in the kitchen with a batch of cookies when the kids came home from school, or Ward Cleaver walked in the front door after an eight-hour day at the office. It is impossible to return to those days.

Today fewer and fewer wives stay home—22 percent, according to the latest census figures, which is a drastic change from 61 percent just thirty years ago. The size of families is smaller, too, with the typical family just 3.2 people. I love that statistic, because I've wondered who that two-tenths of a person could be!

Although I've never been big on statistics, it startled me to read that among first-time mothers under age thirty in America, 40 percent are not married.[4]

As I thought about what is called the "new American family," I realized that Roy's and my own family, four-generational as it is, falls into all of the categories. Divorced, single-parent, career woman, two-career parent, stay-at-home mom—I've been them all. As the old cracker-barrel poet Edgar Guest said, "It takes a heap o' livin' in a house t' make it home." And I guess you could say we've done a heap o' livin'.

Pressure Cooker Families

Carole and I were talking about our early marriage days, and she told me that the only way she knew how to cook then was with a pressure cooker. During World War II, when meat rationing was in effect, her father gave the newlyweds a choice sirloin steak as a present. You guessed it—Carole put it in the pressure cooker. If you know anything about cooking, you know that would turn sirloin into shoe leather.

Today we have good quality men, women, and children who are dumped into this pressure cooker society. No wonder we explode under stress. Our spouses urge us to spend more time with them. Our children tease us to play. Our boss demand we work faster and more efficiently. Our church desires us to be available for committees. Our community pleads for us to be involved with local projects. Television shows, magazines, and billboards implore us to have more money, more power, more sex. People try to do too much and end up neglecting priorities.

This pressure is revealed in the choice of seminars many choose to go to: time management or "How to Organize Your Life." I am not a completely organized person myself but I have learned how to live a pressure cooker life by depending on God's wisdom and power.

Pressure itself is not bad. We would never see a diamond unless a piece of coal had been pressurized. We would never have achievers or champions if there were no pressure. J. Hudson Taylor, missionary to China, said, "As long as the pressure does not come between me and my Savior, but presses me to Him, then the greater the pressure, the greater my dependence upon Him."

Handling pressure does not necessarily mean slowing down. I have known people who accomplish more in less time, simply because they do not major in minors. One minister I know will skip a committee meeting because one of his children is playing in a school game. A couple in a two-career family said they have become "social nerds," turning down most invitations for social functions so they can concentrate on what's more important at this point in their lives.

The problem comes, however, when Christians are too pressured to take their burdens to the Lord. When this happens, we fail to tap into the greatest power source we have. Who would think of having a houseful of electrical appliances and not plugging them in?

We all spend so much time on self-improvement and self-fulfillment that we become self-absorbed. The happiest people I know, even those with pressurized lies, are those who are first God-directed, then others-centered.

All of my life I have been a hurry-up woman. The only

way I have slowed down is when the Lord has said, "Stop." And that is more frequent lately. It has given me a chance to think and evaluate some of the lessons of life.

The Buck Stops Here

One thing I've noticed is that we are so quick to blame others for the erosion of family values. One of our favorite targets is the educational system. As I was twirling my pencil over a yellow pad, ready to send some notes to Carole for this chapter, I grabbed my tape recorder instead and began to reminisce.

Shortly after Roy and I were married and living in Hollywood, we became close friends with a woman who was an informant for our government in the days when "communist leanings" were suspected. She lived next door to an internationally known singer whose family leaned toward the left; consequently, she had made interesting observations about inroads this extremely liberal family had made into the school system.

At the PTA meetings our friend, the government agent, attended, our U.S. history books were under attack. The communist sympathizers wanted any hardwon U.S. victories either soft-pedaled or deleted. These people were strong, influential, and vocal. The parents who valued the true record didn't stand up against them and were outnumbered. The erosion began in our history books. We are all at fault for not standing up for our values. We assumed for years that history stood as true and validated and it would always be that way. Not so.

We are getting exactly what we deserve, since we took the easy way of buckling under to those who wanted to alter the American way to their way.

Even teaching methods have contributed to the downgrading of our children's education. Phonics is not the prevalent method to teach reading anymore; rather, in many cases, systems called "whole language" are being used. As a result, we are graduating functionally illiterate students from our schools. Granted, they are far ahead of us in technology, but are they learning to think out a problem or do they simply depend on computers?

Whole books are written about literacy, and that is not my purpose here. But I do want to say that without a generation who can read with understanding, how can we grow and flourish? My hat is off to Barbara Bush and the impetus she gave to the literacy movement. Some of the greatest family values are learned when children are cuddled on their mother's or father's lap with a book in their hands.

Value of a Christian Heritage

In one of our photo albums is a picture of me at age five, sitting before a huge American flag in front of my grandparents' home in Uvalde, Texas. I was taught at an early age to love and respect our flag because of what it stands for. Since I spent a lot of time in Uvalde, I was also taught to respect the Alamo in San Antonio because of the sacrifices made there. Any Texan knows that the rallying cry, "Remember the Alamo!" is a symbol of courage and sacrifice.

My grandfather Wood was my hero. He was a tall, angular Texan and represented to me everything a grandfather should be. He was painfully honest, as the following story will show.

I remember how he insisted that my mother accompany him to the railroad ticket agency to repay what he thought my mother owed. My brother was a sickly child and very small for a five-year-old. He was ill when we traveled by train from Memphis to Uvalde and spent most of the trip sitting on Mama's lap. She didn't buy him a half-price ticket.

"But, Papa, I held him most of the way, and besides, they would never believe he is five years old."

"Daughter," Grandfather Wood said, "we will not defraud the railroad. We are paying for a half ticket."

My mother applied Grandfather's teaching of love for the Lord, honesty, and patriotism to my brother and me. I know the value of the proverb, "Train up a child in the way he should go, And when he is old he will not depart from it" (Prov. 22:6). I was thirty-five and my brother was forty when we returned to the precepts of her teaching, which she had learned at the feet of Grandfather and Grandmother Wood.

Early-taught values really do pay off later.

Grandfather Wood also believed in the free enterprise system. He did not believe in going into debt. He said, "If you have to sell the shirt off your back to pay your debts, you do it." He also believed that bankruptcy was a disgrace.

He was a poor boy with a fourth-grade education, but he educated eight children through college and left a sizable estate at his death.

Although we are new creatures when we become Christians, I also believe that genetic tendencies are important. One of my forefathers was jailed for preaching the gospel instead of adhering to the dictates of the Church of England. He did street preaching, drawing quite a crowd around him. When he was jailed, he didn't stop. He preached from his jailhouse window to people down below. His genes are strong in me. Since making Jesus Christ my Lord as well as Savior, I believe his heritage is partly responsible for my forthright declaration of Christian faith in the midst of a show business career, even at the expense of a contract.

Building on the Rock

The Lord has told us to build our homes on solid rock. As the old hymn says, "All other ground is sinking sand."

If we have a spiritual heritage, we have a firm foundation to withstand the turmoil around us. We won't be blown away when the storms break loose … as they will.

Billy Graham's daughter, Gigi, wrote a delightful book to celebrate Billy and Ruth's golden wedding anniversary. In part of it, though, she soberly observed:

> *It is frightening when you think about the lack of family role models today. My children look around them and just shake their heads. They have been disillusioned again and again when Christian couples and families they had admired and looked up to are shattered by unfaithfulness and divorce.*
>
> *Where do we look for this Christian heritage we long to pass on to the next generation?*[5]

Where *do* we look? We must look to the Lord to build our families. He will never disappoint us. He will never give us bad advice. He will never abandon us. He is our heritage. We have been adopted by him: "You received the Spirit of adoption by whom we cry out, 'Abba, Father.' The Spirit Himself bears witness with our spirit that we are children of God, and if children, then heirs—heirs of God and joint heirs with Christ" (Rom. 8:15–17).

People can write books, give sermons, and make speeches about family values, but we've heard enough of those. In our society that is struggling from blow after blow against our very foundation we need lived-out examples of good family life, not just words.

Every believer has a rich family heritage. If you don't find good examples in your own family, then look to the family of believers down through the generations. Better yet, let your family heritage start with you! Begin today to pass on new values to your children and grandchildren. Hebrews 12 says we are surrounded by a great cloud of witnesses who cheer us on in this endurance race we call life. So how can we lose?

I remember the times when Roy and I rode Trigger and Buttermilk, our horses, in parades. Children would line the sidewalks and cheer wildly as we waved at them along the route. Their enthusiasm was all the encouragement we needed. No wonder Jesus said, "Let the little children come to me." They are fresh vessels, waiting to be filled by someone who will show them God's love.

Grown-ups may make a shambles out of a world God intended to be beautiful, but just when we're ready to give up, along come the children, bright-eyed and eager to learn. We older blunderers take hope and go on with the fight for a new generation.

When I begin to get depressed at the erosion of bibli-cal family values, I realize I must stop and remember that God is in charge. He is able to heal our families with his love.

7

Value of Friendships

*There is a friend who
sticks closer than a brother.*
Proverbs 18:24

A recent movie was called *A Few Good Men*. In my life I have been privileged to have many friends, but in every life there are just "a few good friends." Usually, the Lord provides them at just the times we need them most.

Charles Spurgeon was called "the prince of preachers," and his grasp of the Scriptures and deep love for Christ infused his sermons and books, which are quoted in evangelical churches throughout the world. In a book on meditations, he wrote this:

> *Friendship is the only thing in the world concerning
> the usefulness of which all mankind are agreed.
> Friendship seems as necessary an element of a
> comfortable existence in this world as fire and water,*

or even air itself. A man may drag along a miserable existence in proud solitary dignity, but his life is scarce life; it is nothing but an existence, the tree of life being stripped of the leaves of hope and the fruits of joy. **He who would be happy here must have friends; and he who would be happy hereafter must above all things, find a friend in the world to come, in the person of God, the Father of His people** *(author's emphasis).*[1]

Why Some People Don't Have Friends

One of the most friendless men in America was also one of the richest men in the world. In his later years, Howard Hughes led a life of such lunacy that most of us could not understand. His physical appearance became so bizarre that he must have been repulsive to all of the people who were paid to care for him. His beard hung down to his waist, and his fingernails were like claws. Hughes was only interested in airplanes, technology, and making money. There were no great eulogies when he died.

Some people don't have friends because they are so caught up in the superficial life of parties, social engagements, and work that they don't take time to cultivate deep, lasting friendships. It's been said that God gave us things to use and people to enjoy. People without friends use people and enjoy things.

Some people don't have friends because qualities in their personalities are objectionable. Too loud. Too manipulating. Too critical. Too sarcastic. Too self-pitying. Perhaps we all have one or more of those traits at some time. But they sure don't need to be permanent.

Just consider some of Jesus' followers. James and John, the sons of Zebedee, were selfish and wanted to sit next to Jesus in places of honor. They did not endear themselves to the other ten disciples any more than the person who shoves ahead of us in line. Peter might have destroyed a precious friendship when he denied knowing Jesus. Nathanael was sarcastic. "Can anything good come out of Nazareth?" (John 1:46). Saul was brutal and ruthless before he met Christ on the road to Damascus. Mark skipped out on his friends and went home without an explanation.

Whenever someone says, "That's just the way I am," wait. Remember, you don't have to stay in a ditch just because you fell in it.

"When someone becomes a Christian he becomes a brand new person inside. He is not the same any more. A new life has begun!" (2 Cor. 5:17 LB).

To Be a Friend ... and Have Friends

While we were writing this chapter, dancer Gene Kelly died. To Sherman White, a soundman who worked on

Kelly's films, his death meant more than a loss of a great talent. It was the passing of a man who knew the value of friendship.

"Gene was a great fella," White told a reporter. "He was everybody's friend. He was just the guy next door, except he had a tremendous talent."

White ended the interview by adding, "If you have real, great, honest-to-God character, like Jimmy Stewart or Gene Kelly, you go out gracefully."[2]

Ralph Waldo Emerson said, "The only reward of virtue is virtue; the only way to have a friend is to be one."

Many today don't know how to be a friend. To be a friend, we should dare to say, "I love you." Some people choke on those words as if they were cod liver oil. Love is the basis of all friendships, and without it we only have people who gallop through our lives without stopping to graze and enjoy the view. Why do we need to have principles and guidelines for relationships that should be as natural as breathing? Perhaps it's because we have been programmed to "look out for number one." Howard Hughes did that, and look where it got him.

Carole told me about a business seminar she attended where the main speaker broke down on stage after telling a story about his father. For the first time in that man's life, his father told him that he loved him. The man was fifty-seven years old. My parents never ceased to tell me they loved me, no matter how wayward I was. Jesus never ceases to love me, just as I am. When we sing, "What a friend I have in Jesus," we're singing about the ultimate friendship. Jesus is our example of real love. He has said, "I love you," in countless ways.

To be a friend, be cautious in criticism. When someone says, "This is for your own good," I wonder what good will come of it. D. L. Moody was a great evangelist and preacher. One of his famous sayings was, "Right now I'm having so much trouble with D. L. Moody that I don't have time to find fault with the other fellow."

Years ago I wrote a book called *My Spiritual Diary*. When you write a book, appear before an audience, or have a position of influence in any field, you will be criticized. It's been said that the farther up the ladder you climb, the easier it is for people to take potshots at you. One day I wrote this story in that diary:

> *Our good friends, Dr. Norman Vincent Peale, and Frank Mead and Wilbur Davies of the Fleming Revell Company have just left. What a delightful time we had together. We talked of the trials and tribulations of being a Christian in these days and we had a good laugh over a lot of them. These men have a great sense of humor. They can laugh off the most devastating criticism of their books and sermons, and that is a gift straight from God! They are serious enough when the criticism is important, but stupid*

or intolerant criticism they throw off like so many ducks shedding water off their backs. I cherish the gift of good humor in the faith. There would be a lot fewer spiritual casualties if we had more of it.

We discussed the problem of publishing religious books—of how hard it is to get a book published that will find any audience at all, with people in the churches so divided and quarreling among themselves.

Dr. Peale has the answer, I think. He says, "Write what God gives you to write, and forward all letters of criticism to Him!"[3]

Wouldn't it be great to hand over criticism to the Lord instead of letting it fester in our hearts? Someone once said that constructive criticism is when I criticize you. Destructive criticism is when you criticize me.

To be a friend, be an encourager. When Robin died, the floodgates of care and encouragement opened. The Eilers family—Frances, Leonard, and Joy—came to the house and waited until Robin's little body was taken away and stayed with me and let me cry. I'm so grateful they didn't say, "Now, now, don't cry." They put their arms around me and let me pour it all out. That's friendship.

Some people are just natural encouragers, it seems. They send a note of congratulation or consolation. They bring food when you can't cook for yourself. They keep quiet when you need to talk.

Rich DeVos, cofounder of the Amway corporation, with twelve thousand employees and two million distributors, was asked, "How do you lead such a vast organization?" DeVos answered, "Oh, I'm not a leader; I'm just a cheerleader."

Good friends are good encouragers, but the greatest encouragement of all is in the Book. "For everything that was written in the past was written to teach us, so that through endurance and the *encouragement of the Scriptures we might have hope"* (Rom. 15:4 NIV, emphasis added).

Friends accept us just as we are. This does not mean they approve of everything. Acceptance is a different matter. When I hear the song, "Just As I Am" sung as an invitation, I know that God hasn't asked us to clean up our act before we accept him. Good friends see our shortcomings and love us anyhow.

The Bible says, "Therefore encourage one another and build each other up" (1 Thess. 5:11 NIV).

The Power in a Touch

A friend can boost your day with a pat on the back or a hug. I believe we all need at least eight hugs a day. The way to get them is to give them. Hugs between friends are a way of saying, "You're special to me," "I've missed you," or "We both need a boost."

We wither without the touch of caring hands. A computer instructor was teaching a class on the use of the more sophisticated methods of accessing information. He bragged about the prowess of his three-year-old daughter, who knew how to turn on a computer and find special pictures and games she could play by herself. Her father said, "She's learning to read by CD-ROM." What happens to the wonderful closeness that comes when a child sits on Daddy's or Mommy's lap and is read to from books? Computers cannot cuddle or hug.

Jesus used the power of touch to cure a man of leprosy, to raise Peter's mother-in-law from her sickbed, to take the children in his arms. The touch of Jesus can touch and heal anyone. It did me.

Friends Listen

A psychiatrist said that patients come to his office because they know so few people who will genuinely listen to what they are saying. Good listeners listen with their eyes, not just their ears. When someone looks around the room or glances sideways to make sure he doesn't miss someone more important, you know he isn't listening. I have often heard in my life, "Grandma, watch me." We are not listening unless we are watching.

Alan Loy McGinnis, in his book *The Friendship Factor,* tells a story about Lincoln during the darkest hours of the Civil War. The president sent for an old friend and fellow lawyer to come to Washington because he wanted to discuss some problems.

The friend, Leonard Swett, hurried to the White House, and Lincoln talked to him for hours about the arguments pro and con for freeing the slaves. Lincoln did all the talking himself. Swett went back to Illinois without even giving his opinion. All Lincoln wanted was a friendly, sympathetic listener.

For thirty years we have had a friend who has listened to many of our joys and triumphs. He is Bill Hansen, the minister of our church. When we first moved to Apple Valley, we visited the church where he preached to see if we liked it. Bill was never without a smile. I thought, *Is this just a façade?* So I went back again. His smile was always there and it was real. That smile and his listening ear have sustained us through many experiences.

Jesus was a great conversationalist, but he was also a very attentive listener. He asked questions of Roman officers, blind men, rabbis, fishermen, mothers, religious zealots, rich people, common people. We call him a Great Teacher, but he was also a Great Listener.

Friends Share Joys and Sorrows

I received a wedding invitation that said, "This day I will marry my friend, the one I laugh with, dream with, love…" Isn't that great? I wish more people would fall in friend before they fall in love. Roy and I had a friendship that grew into love. I believe friendship is the basic ingredient for a good marriage.

Women have more close friends than men, and I've often wondered why. Little girls walk to school together holding hands and say, "She's my best friend." Little boys punch and cuff each other as a sign of friendship. Girls love to have slumber parties and tell secrets. Boys like to go into the woods and play "search and rescue." When they grow up, the same trend continues. Women's friendships revolve around sharing; men's revolve around activities.

When I was making pictures at Republic Studios, I had a double, Alice Van. When there was a long shot on a horse, Alice rode. She took some of my falls for me. Alice was a world-championship trick rider and the first woman to acquire a horse-training license in the state of Illinois. During the time we worked together, we both had sons who lived with our parents. We had a lot in common.

Alice and I are still close friends. She is like a sister to me. No matter how far away we may live, when we get together it's like yesterday. Friendships like that are not developed overnight.

Memories of good friends never fade. My agent, Art Rush, has gone to be with the Lord, but I shall never forget his friendship. When our dearest Debbie was killed in the school bus accident and Roy was seriously ill in the hospital, all of the arrangements were left to me. Art was there, helping me make decisions, doing all of the little chores that needed to be done. He never asked, "What can I do?" He just did them.

When I talk about my friends, I wonder how people can manage without friends of their own. The only thing that has sustained me has been my wonderful friend Jesus and those precious people he has brought into my life.

An unknown poet wrote these words:

When trouble comes your soul to try,
You love the friend who just stands by.
Perhaps there's nothing he can do;
The thing is strictly up to you,
For there are troubles all your own,
And paths the soul must tread alone;
Times when love can't smooth the road,
Nor friendship lift the heavy load.

But just to feel you have a friend,
Who will stand by until the end;
Whose sympathy through all endures,
Whose warm handclasp is always yours.
It helps somehow to pull you through,
Although there's nothing he can do;
And so with fervent heart we cry,
"God bless the friend who just stands by."[4]

The Bible says: "A friend loves at all times" (Prov. 17:17 NIV).

8

Value of Discipline

Blessed is the man
you discipline, O LORD.

Psalm 94:12 NIV

*G*od has disciplined me for the past thirty-five years. I admit I haven't enjoyed being taken to the woodshed. However, I know that without his discipline I would be like one of those little windup toys that spins and spins out of control.

In Eugene Peterson's paraphrase of the Bible, the writer of Hebrews reminds us:

So don't feel sorry for yourselves. Or have you
forgotten how good parents treat children, and
*that God regards you as **his** children?*

"My dear child, don't shrug off God's discipline,
but don't be crushed by it either.
It's the child he loves that he disciplines;
the child he embraces, he also corrects."

God is educating you; that's why you must never drop
out. He's treating you as dear children. This trouble
*you're in isn't punishment, it's **training**, the normal*
experience of children. Only irresponsible parents
leave children to fend for themselves. Would you
prefer an irresponsible God? (Heb. 12:5–7)[1]

In the past few decades, personal discipline seems to have taken a backseat to "do your own thing." Frank Sinatra had his eightieth birthday recently. A special celebration was held in a large theater and televised for millions. It seemed to me that the biggest and longest ovation was for his rendition of "My Way." When Sinatra sings, "I did it my way," he brings out our independent spirit. It's the child in us who says, "Please, Mother, let me do it myself."

For a Christian, discipline or self-control means we choose God's way instead of insisting on having our own way.

Many times I've stood in church and sung, "Take my life, and let it be consecrated Lord to Thee." Through the hymn we continue to give our moments, our hands, our feet, our voice, our lips, our intellect, our will, our heart, our love, and, finally, ourselves. That's a tall order. If we give our lives to Jesus Christ, he has the right to discipline us his way.

Enemies of Discipline

Laziness and emotionalism are two of the greatest enemies of discipline. Lazy people can't be bothered to acquire disciplined habits in life. A friend of mine has a big card on her refrigerator that says, "Procrastination is the thief of success." We often fall into the Scarlett O'Hara complex: "I'll think about it tomorrow."

If an athlete puts off training because she is tired, she could lose in the competition. If a businessman doesn't answer phone calls, he might find himself without clients. If an actress parties all night and doesn't learn her lines, she's out of a job. If a student doesn't study, he will flunk.

The principle of self-discipline is this: "Do what needs to be done when it ought to be done, whether you like it or not."

Disciplining ourselves is often difficult because we take on the whole task all at once, get discouraged, and give up. But if we took just one step at a time, we'd soon know the sweetness of success. For example, in writing a book, I put one word at a time on the page. In studying a script, I can only memorize one side (a half page) at a time. And a marathon racer takes one mile at a time.

Emotional people who live by their feelings also struggle with self-discipline. To say, "Well, I'll do it if I feel like it," is the opposite of a disciplined life. With that attitude we would only read the Bible and pray when we felt like it. We would go to church only on the days we felt like it. But if we only went to work on the days we felt like it, we would not keep a job. Should we give our Lord any less service than we give our earthly employer?

When Robin was alive, I developed self-discipline by necessity. I was working five and six days a week and had a home and family to manage. To discipline myself to find time alone was important for my sanity. I did a lot of praying in my car and between scenes on the set. I learned to talk less, which for a woman who loves to gab is a real challenge.

Today I have to discipline myself because my health is not very good. I need to stretch and do my exercises every morning and night. When Carole called to ask me some questions about this subject, she said, "What is the most difficult area of your life to discipline?" That caught me off guard. I said, "It's trying not to become irritated when I get constant interruptions."

It was quiet on the other end of the line. "Do you mean like this phone call?"

We had a good laugh.

Luck Is a Loser

Joy Eilers is a dear friend who has accompanied me on the piano for many television programs. She plays so effortlessly that she makes it look easy. Some might say, "I wish I could play like Joy." They don't mean it, though. If they did, they would have practiced every day since they were a child, even when they didn't feel like it.

We call people "natural" athletes, but these talents come from hours and years of training. Take away the discipline of mind and body from an athlete and you have a loser.

Success has its price.

The Dennis Byrd story is an inspiring example of discipline and determination. From the time he was a child, Dennis wanted to play football. He finally made it as one of the game's leading defensive linemen with the New York Jets. During one game, he collided with a 280-pound teammate, and his neck was broken.

Doctors said he would be paralyzed from the neck down for life. But they underestimated Dennis and his personal relationship with Jesus. In the grueling weeks of rehabilitation, which took more discipline than football training ever did, Dennis defied the negative prognosis and walked out of the hospital. Today he is coaching high school football in Oklahoma.

Hold Your Horses

We were in St. Louis for a rodeo sponsored by the firemen of that city. When Roy galloped into the arena and Trigger saluted the crowd by standing on his rear legs, the place went wild. How many hours of disciplined training do you think it took to perfect that trick? I can't even guess. Horses are like children—they will run wild if not disciplined.

We have had many dogs, and Roy spent untold hours training them to be good hunters. Now that we are unable to make the effort to discipline dogs, we own cats. If anyone knows the method to discipline a cat, please give me the secret. You don't own cats; they own you.

If we discipline our pets, should we do any less with our children? Should God do any less with his children?

Train Up a Child

When someone mentions discipline, most people think of children. Perhaps it is because that is where discipline should start. Undisciplined adults were undoubtedly undisciplined children.

When we were living in Encino, California, it was my habit to do one big shopping trip every two weeks. Dodie was about two years old when we went on one of these major expeditions. (Dear mothers, I know what it is like to shop with children in tow. It takes courage.)

Our cart was groaning with groceries, and Dodie was perched in the seat in the front of the basket. She began to demand chewing gum in a tone loud enough for the butcher in the back of the store to hear. I said "no," and she raised her voice another decibel. Actually, she was howling. I lifted her out of the cart, put her over my leg, and gave her a few choice whacks on her backside. Then I put her back in the seat and proceeded through the checkout line. Every parent who has ever had to discipline a child in a public place knows the feeling. You want to be invisible until your child is a perfect little cherub.

A lady shopper (probably a Dr. Spock follower) said so I could hear, "I've never seen anything so disgusting in my life."

I smiled and answered, "I'll bet she'll never do it again." And she didn't.

A pastor in Santa Barbara caused a stir of controversy by suggesting that the best way to prevent young children from joining gangs is an old-fashioned spanking. Reverend Richard Ramos works with a group that deals with drug prevention. He was quoted as saying, "I know this isn't going to make me popular with some parents ... but this is one father who does not believe that spanking my children is an act of violence."

Ramos suggested spanking two- to ten-year-olds for open defiance or to punish them for having a rebellious attitude. He also recommended spanking before the parent gets angry, using one to three swats with the hand on the buttocks only, and spanking hard enough that the child remembers or cries.[2]

Where were you, Reverend Ramos, when I was in the grocery store with Dodie?

Ann Landers answers letters from her readers with a lot of wisdom. One woman wrote about visiting a state park and stopping to take pictures of her six-year-old daughter and two-year-old son standing next to two life-size dinosaur models. These giant figures were roped off and signs proclaimed, Do Not Touch the Models. Other families were there with their children, who were going under the ropes and climbing on the models to pose for pictures.

The behavior of the children who were allowed to do what they wanted, in spite of warning signs, infuriated the letter writer. She said in a loud voice to her husband, "What good children we have, honey! They can't read the posters, but they know that a rope means 'Do not touch.'" The other parents gave her ugly looks and continued to take pictures.

The writer also told about going to a restaurant where children at a nearby table were spitting drinks at each other through straws, getting those at the writer's table wet. The parents ignored complaints and said, "They're just having fun, nothing personal."

Landers was asked, "What are these parents teaching their children?"

Her reply was: "Those parents are teaching their children it's OK to ignore signs posted for their own safety, and if it's fun to do something, go ahead and do it, even though it interferes with the comfort or well-being of others. I pity those children. They are starting out in life with a lot of baggage. It's going to be a rough journey."[3]

When our children were young, we disciplined them

with spankings and when they were older, by withdraw-ing privileges. Our children knew without a shadow of a doubt that we loved them. In later years Dusty said, "Mom, you ruined our discipline by saying you were sorry. You had to discipline us. We needed it."

If I ruined their discipline, the results don't show it. They turned out real good.

I frequently misbehaved as a child. (That's a conserv-ative statement!) I knew what a spanking meant but I also knew that my parents would be merciful when they saw any sign of repentance.

One time I was told to help my little brother throw some bricks over a fence in our backyard. That wasn't my idea of fun; I wanted to play with my dolls. In a fit of defi-ance, I threw a brick that hit the fence and bounced back on my brother's head. The blood rushed out of a deep gash in his forehead. I ran screaming into the house, "I've killed my little brother!"

Mama and Daddy came out running, applied a ban-dage to Hillman, and called the doctor. I fully expected a whipping. I didn't mean to hurt him, and my parents knew it, so they let discipline take care of itself.

Proper Discipline Is Not Abuse

Our nation is full of horrific stories of child abuse. In my book *Hear the Children Crying,* I said, "I firmly believe that it is sometimes almost impossible for a parent to know where to draw the line between punishment and abuse, unless that parent has a strong religious faith."[4]

Discipline must always be done with love and never in the heat of anger. A child must know the boundaries of good and bad conduct and know the consequences of stepping out of those boundaries (just as the children who ducked under the ropes around the dinosaurs should have been pulled back by their parents).

Even an animal is safer and happier with a loving master to train him.

The permissiveness of the past is reaping the criminals of the present. When Dr. James Dobson was asked to define "permissiveness," he said, "I refer to the absence of effective parental authority, resulting in the lack of boundaries for the child. This word represents childish disrespect, defiance, and the general confusion that occurs in the absence of adult leadership."[5]

It has been said that it is less painful to discipline a child than to weep over a spoiled youth.

Which will we choose, Americans: discipline or despair?

9

Value of Patience

My brethren, count it all joy
when you fall into various trials,
knowing that the testing of your faith
produces patience.

James 1:2–3

Teri had a frantic day. Her second-grader had missed the bus, and she had to take her to school. No time to dress, so she went in her bathrobe, buckled the baby in his car seat (dirty diaper and all), and arrived just as the bell rang. The president of the PTA spied her and rushed over to the car to talk. Teri had to roll down the window and reveal her charming image and the interior of the odor-filled car.

The day continued to deteriorate.

The sink overflowed when she answered the phone and forgot to turn off the water.

The baby wouldn't take a nap.

Her oldest child came home with a D in geometry and slammed the door so hard that the crystal vase on the shelf fell off and scattered glass on the hall floor.

The cat got a sliver of glass in his paw and howled until Teri got the tweezers to pull it out. That ungrateful cat scratched her hand.

Milk spilled, cookies burned, phone rang, supper was unplanned. One look in the mirror confirmed that this was a bad hair day.

Teri slumped in a kitchen chair to write a grocery list at 5 P.M. and prayed the great American prayer: "Lord, give me patience ... right now."

No one's life is the same as another's, but I can empathize with a day like Teri's. It seems as if I put too much on my platter every day. I cram too much into a crowded schedule and then want it done yesterday. I get antsy inside and feel like I'm being pushed. The person who is pushing, however, is looking at me in the mirror.

When a child wants Christmas or her birthday to come tomorrow, we say, "Be patient." When someone honks the horn for us to hurry, we mutter, "Why can't he be patient?"

Patience is a virtue, but for many of us it does not come easily.

Wait Here

One of the hardest lessons to learn in life is patience. Waiting for a child in the high chair to eat may be an endurance contest. To listen without interrupting to the stories of a long-winded friend or someone who details every scene from a movie qualifies us for sainthood.

To "wait upon the Lord," though, may be the greatest test of patience given to us.

During Robin's short lifetime, I was asked by many magazine editors to write an article about what it was like to have a child with Down's syndrome. I promised the Lord and those editors that someday I would. "When the time is right."

The day after Robin's funeral, I was looking at her lovely little face in a picture on my desk. I was dazed and numb with grief. Endless calls of sympathy came from our friends, which provided some distraction from the ache inside me. Suddenly, thoughts came into my mind so fast that I picked up a pencil and started to write. My hand finally became cramped, and I couldn't write anymore.

Roy and I had contracted months before to do a dramatic program for Dodge Motors on NBC and shortly afterwards a show in Madison Square Garden. When I wasn't on mike and had a few moments to rest, I thought about Robin's story. Why couldn't I continue it? I closed my eyes and started to pray, and the answer came so clearly, *Let Robin write it*. I was letting my feelings, my grief, interfere with the message. *Let her speak for herself and others who are handicapped like she was.*

I picked up a pen again and began to write every waking moment. On the train to New York I wrote and wrote. By the time we pulled into Grand Central Station, the little book was finished. It had been just six weeks since Robin went to be with the Lord.

Now what do I do, Lord?

I wasn't really sure of my direction; it was just the echo of my heartbreak that drove me. I took my notes and walked over to Central Park and sat on a stone bench next to the zoo. Patience, Dale, patience.

I bowed my head and just kept saying over and over, "Thy will be done, thy will be done. Please tell me if this is of you. Lord. Please tell me."

When I looked up, I saw a woman coming toward me with a Down's syndrome little girl. I knew that God had spoken to me, because at that time people didn't take those children out for public view. I fairly ran back to the hotel and burst into our suite. "Roy, he did it! God spoke to me about Robin's book!"

Dear, patient Roy had suffered as much as I had over Robin's death, but he sustained and supported me in my weakness.

I pulled together all the scraps of paper I had written in the past few weeks. Out of those tearstained notes that I had finished on the train came a little book … *Angel Unaware*. It was Robin's book and God's book, not mine. I was merely the hand he used. Now what do I do with it, Lord?

Again, it was as if the Lord directed me to pick up the phone and call Marble Collegiate Church and ask for an appointment with Dr. Norman Vincent Peale. He had written a chapter in his book *Guide to Confident Living* on "How to Meet Sorrow." When I read it, I thought that someday I wanted to thank him.

As secretaries are prone to do, she told me how busy he was, how people made appointments weeks ahead, etcetera. Fifteen minutes later I walked into his office. This time God hadn't told me to wait.

Dr. Peale was a kind and wise man. We prayed together on our knees, and then I read to him what God had directed me to write. He didn't say a word all through the reading. When I finished, he looked at me with tears in his eyes and said, "It's beautiful. I will help you get it published."

My impatient nature had been bridled until I learned to wait on the Lord's direction.

Patience When Nothing Seems to Be Happening

Sometimes we pray and wait and nothing happens. Why does God take so long? Satan, in the subtle way he can use, begins to play with our thoughts. We begin to condemn ourselves.

Maybe I don't deserve an answer. Doubts begin to cloud our thinking.

Maybe God hasn't heard me. Impatience overwhelms us.

I've waited so long, maybe God just wants me to go ahead and solve this problem on my own. Ego and pride dominate us.

With instant credit, fast food, freeways, jet travel, and now cyberspace, we in America are not prone to patience. Yet the Word of God has a lot to say about waiting.

When Pharaoh of Egypt died, the children of Israel groaned and cried because they wanted out of their slavery. Forty years later, God sent Moses to lead them out of Egypt.

Samuel anointed David king when David was just a boy, but it was another ten or fifteen years before he was finally crowned.

Jesus was twelve years old when he stayed in the temple, asking and answering questions. When he was found by his parents, he returned to Nazareth, and eighteen years passed before he began his public ministry.

We are so impatient to have everything happen *right now.*

Isaiah's words help me realize that God is not punishing us by making us wait; rather, God's timing is gracious. "Therefore the LORD will wait, that He may be gracious to you; and therefore He will be exalted, that He may have mercy on you. For the LORD is a God of justice; blessed are all those who wait for Him" (Isa. 30:18).

God's Stretching

One of my favorite devotionals is Oswald Chambers' *My Utmost for His Highest.* Chambers died in 1917 at the age of forty-three but he still speaks to millions today. Every time I pick up his little book, I marvel that one person could have such insight into the deep truths of the Word. When I nestle into my recliner, with our cat on my lap and Chambers' book in my hand, it's like exploring the deep things of God with an old friend. He writes:

> *Patience is more than endurance. A saint's life is in the hands of God like a bow and arrow in the hands of an archer. God is aiming at something the saint cannot see, and He stretches and strains, and every now and again the saint says— "I cannot stand any more." God does not heed. He goes on stretching till His purpose is in sight, then He lets fly. Trust yourself in God's hands. For what have you need of patience just now? Maintain your relationship to Jesus Christ by the patience of faith. "Though He slay me, yet will I wait for Him."*[1]

Most of us have seen enough cowboy and Indian movies or watched *Robin Hood* to know how far back the archer pulls the bow before letting go. If the bow could talk, it might say, "Ouch, I've had enough ... let me loose." Many times in my life I've felt like shouting, *Enough is enough! I can't take any more of this pain!*

When I had my most severe heart attack, it felt like knives were piercing my body. I cried, "Lord, was it like this for you on the cross?" Then I remembered that the Bible said he "endured the cross" (Heb. 12:2).

Endurance is the most intense form of patience.

Waiting Isn't Easy

Anyone who has flown enough to accumulate thousands of those frequent flyer miles knows the frustrations you can encounter at an airport or aboard the plane. We've been in scenes like these. The plane is two hours late. People are grumpy and some are downright mad, letting everyone else know how they feel. Flight attendants are apologizing and trying to keep a positive attitude. When we are finally in the sky, a baby is screaming from the pressure. The meal is late and less than palatable. The lady next to us has a cold and is wearing heavy perfume. The movie has embarrassing scenes, and we worry about the children who are watching.

It's times like these that no one cares if I've written Christian books or have appeared in the movies. All they see is how we react. Are we calm? Smiling? Without irritation?

Did we remember that "the fruit of the Spirit is love, joy, peace, *patience* ... " (Gal. 5:22 NIV)?

David was not always a patient man. In Psalm 69 he wrote: "Save me, O God! For the waters have come up to my neck. I sink in deep mire, Where there is no standing; I have come into deep waters, Where the floods overflow me. I am weary with my crying; My throat is dry; My eyes fail while I wait for my God" (vv. 1–3).

It certainly sounds as if David was in trouble. Later on he wrote, "Hear me speedily" (v. 17). Again, in Psalm 70 he pleaded, "Make haste, O God, to deliver me! Make haste to help me, O LORD!" (v. 1).

Isn't it gratifying to know that the great King David was just like us? "Hurry up, God, I'm tired of waiting!"

And yet God says to us:

> *But those who wait on the LORD shall renew their strength; they shall mount up with wings like eagles, they shall run and not be weary, they shall walk and not faint (Isa. 40:31).*

(My favorite verse.)

Teach me, Lord, to Wait for Your Power

When Debbie and her girlfriend were killed in that church bus crash in 1964, I needed the Lord's super-spiritual strength. Roy was hospitalized from a spinal fusion. He had been dangerously ill and was in no shape to help with the details of the funeral. To top it off, the press monopolized my phone, and I couldn't even get through to Roy in the hospital.

Debbie's death, Roy's illness, the decisions that had to be made, the pressure of the news media all dealt me a wallop.

I prayed that I would be a witness to the power of the Lord before the people attending the funeral. The Holy Spirit sustained me. God helped me keep my composure in front of all those people. Of course, I fell apart later, but when I needed the strength, he was there.

The Least Dramatic Value

Patience is not very popular today. We feel that the faster we go, the more we accomplish. It seems to be almost a virtue to say, "I'm so busy." We are determined to push everything at breakneck speed.

Roy and I have had a lot of animals during our lifetime. When we get a puppy, it seems like no time before he's grown. A cute little kitten becomes an independent cat in a few months. A baby, on the other hand, takes many years before reaching maturity. Humans take much longer to grow up. God did not design for us to be microwave men and women.

God's work is never hurried. James says, "Let patience have its perfect work" (1:4).

We cannot teach the value of patience in the classroom or from the pulpit. I can write about its value, but they will only be hollow words. Patience is taught in our lives and in our actions.

St. Francis of Assisi wrote: "No one will ever know the full depth of his capacity for patience and humility as long as nothing bothers him. It is only when times are troubled and difficult that he can see how much of either is in him." As the phone interrupts my thoughts again (why don't I have the fortitude to let it ring?), I think, *Oh Lord, teach me to be patient. Right now!*

10

A Call to Valor

Now it came to pass,
when the time had come
for Him to be received up,
that He steadfastly set
His face to go to Jerusalem.

Luke 9:51

*J*esus knew what awaited him at his destination. Mocking, beatings, human cruelty in the extreme. Then, finally, death by crucifixion. Nevertheless, "He steadfastly set His face to go to Jerusalem."

His was the ultimate example of valor.

Courage is exhibited in many ways. Martyrs have shown physical courage that most of us in America cannot comprehend. Stories from the Nazi death camps stagger us with the degree of man's inhumanity to man. From political prisoners in communist Russia to tortured

Christians in Red China, the torment has been beyond what most of us can fathom.

Have we ceased to pray for our suffering brothers and sisters in other parts of the world? We feel so safe inside our churches. The Berlin Wall has fallen. Communism is dead. (Is it?) China has opened its doors to American business and trade. What have we to worry about?

Charles Colson wrote that the Muslim government in Sudan has made it a crime to convert to Christianity. In Sudan, Libya, and other Islamic countries, thousands of women from Christian families have been raped, sold as servants or concubines. Men have been crucified.

Here is a list of places where Christians *today* are being persecuted: Pakistan, Egypt, Saudi Arabia, Iran. There may be more. Colson said,

> Despite the gruesome evidence, the U.S. government inexplicably refuses to recognize what is happening . . . the Immigration and Naturalization Service often denies asylum to victims of anti-Christian terror. The INS even returns them to the countries they have fled—where they face imprisonment, torture, even death—in clear violation of U.S. laws granting asylum to religious refugees.[1]

Our nation was founded by religious believers fleeing persecution. Have we forgotten? Have we learned anything from history? Remember when our American leaders denied there was religious persecution by communist governments? Then Aleksandr Solzhenitsyn's writings were smuggled out of Russia, and the horror of the Gulag Archipelago was revealed. Perhaps some literary genius will wake us up to Islam-inspired terror.

It doesn't take much valor on our part to raise our voices and take up our pens in defense of fellow believers. If we don't stand up for what we believe, we may fall into that indifferent and lukewarm attitude Jesus condemned in the church at Laodicea. He said, "I know your works, that you are neither cold nor hot. I could wish you were cold or hot. So then, because you are lukewarm, and neither cold nor hot, I will spew you out of My mouth" (Rev. 3:15–16).

I would rather be called a firebrand than a wet noodle.

In small ways and large, people of valor set examples that give us courage. Their stories are more inspiring than the lifestyles of the rich and famous.

When Moses handed over the leadership of Israel to Joshua, he said, "Be strong and of good courage, do not fear nor be afraid of them; for the LORD your God, He is the One who goes with you. He will not leave you nor forsake you" (Deut. 31:6).

God speaks to us today and says, "Be strong and of good courage. I will not leave you."

Left for Dead

Korea has forty-three million people, and more than eleven million are professing Christians. Some of the largest churches in the world are located in South Korea. How did Christianity make such a big impact on a country that is predominantly Buddhist? More than anyone else, one man showed the courage to be persecuted for his faith and light the spark of revival.

When the Communists occupied Korea (1950–53), North Korean soldiers began murdering any civilians who disagreed with communist ideology. Dr. Kim saw his father and his wife brutally killed before his eyes. He was beaten by a club and almost had his throat cut with a sword. He was stuffed into a sack to be thrown into the sea from the top of a cliff, but he was miraculously spared at the last minute.

After the war, Kim felt he was called to preach and managed to travel to the United States to study at Fuller Theological Seminary in California. The rest of the story is the astounding history of the formation of Korea Campus Crusade for Christ under the leadership of Dr. Kim. It has been said that he is the key person in the evangelization of Korea, and today there are Korean Christians all over the world who trace their spiritual origin to him.

God's man in Korea could have been thrown over a cliff in a sack.

God's Smuggler

Brother Andrew is a Dutchman who smuggled Bibles behind the Iron Curtain when the penalty for such an act was imprisonment, even death. He experienced fear, just as all of us do. He wrote,

> I've driven toward the Iron Curtain with my carload of Scripture, arrived at the border, seen the controls, and gotten so scared I've turned around and driven back to a hotel in the nearest village where I could pray and fast. I'd stay there until I had faith that with God I was a majority; and that I could cross over with Scripture and preach on the other side and not be caught.[2]

Brother Andrew and his Open Doors ministry have smuggled millions of Bibles into Russia, China, parts of Asia, Africa, Central America, and, finally, the Middle East.

I've never smuggled Bibles or been tortured for Christ, but I've often wondered if we American Christians will ever be called on to face that kind of opposition to our faith.

What More Can Be Said about Billy?

The most admired and respected Christian leader in the world is Billy Graham. He is a man of valor because he is committed to the purity and power of his ministry. Billy has faced death threats, criticism, loneliness, family problems, and financial insecurity. Yet he has never wavered from the task God has called him to do.

In spite of his robust appearance on the podium in front of thousands of people, his most brutal adversary has probably been his poor health. To list the number of ailments he has suffered would look like a page from a first-year medical student's textbook. (I'm not sure of that analogy, because I've never seen a medical student's textbook.) However, he said, "I intend to keep on going, preaching the gospel, writing the gospel, as long as I have any breath. I hope my last word as I am dying—whether by a bullet wound, by cancer, a heart attack, or a stroke— I hope my dying word will be *Jesus*."[3]

In a call to valor, Billy would be on the front lines.

Stand Up, Stand Up for Jesus

Compromise is the opposite of valor. When we are tempted to compromise our faith, it's like Peter denying Christ three times. Christ forgave him and welcomed him back into his inner circle. But I don't believe Peter ever forgot the humiliation of hearing that cock crow.

Yes, I have compromised. I'm just a sinner saved by grace and have had to ask for forgiveness many times. Although I do not want to elevate myself into the same stratosphere as many uncompromising and courageous souls who have been my heroes, I do remember times when God has given me strength to stand up for what I believe.

Roy and I had signed a contract in 1952 to appear in Madison Square Garden. The show was to go on only three weeks after Robin died. Roy and I rode Trigger and Buttermilk into the center of the arena and sang "Peace in the Valley." It took the power of God's peace to get me through that number. Roy had arranged for the arena to be darkened except for a single shaft of light in the form of a huge cross beaming on us as we sang. It was one of those "moments in time."

The manager of Madison Square Garden had a fit. The whole presentation was "too religious," and the cross was offensive.

Roy said, "You will either leave it in or you will find a new cowboy."

A matinee performance was scheduled for the next day, and hundreds of young people were there. When the cross hit the black turf, the place went wild. The kids stamped and cheered until we thought the bleachers would break.

After the show, the manager said, "Okay, leave the cross in."

Another time we did a variety show that was filmed in Seattle. Ralph Carmichael and his orchestra backed us. In one of my numbers, I sang, "When Christ shall come with shout of acclamation."

When the dress rehearsal ended, the producer of the show said, "Tell Dale she has to take out 'Christ.'"

I said, "I will not take Christ out."

The show was canceled after two or three times, and our contract was not renewed. It was too late in the season to get another contract, so we were out of work.

Extremists, Etc.

In football and baseball stadiums, zeal for the sport makes perfect sense. Stand, yell, scream, it's okay. But stand up for God and you'll be labeled. "Right-wing religious extremist" is the latest in name-calling. A little bit of God may be politically correct, they say, but don't go so far as to be called a "religious nut."

When Tom was at USC in a course called "Man and Civilization," he was crestfallen to hear his professor ridicule the Bible. When he had finished his diatribe, the professor said, "Anyone who believes in the Bible, stand up."

Tom and one other boy stood to their feet. "Sir, I know in whom I have believed," Tom said. Bless his heart, I was so proud of him. He even quoted part of a verse that he must have memorized during the years my mother nurtured him. The verse is: "Nevertheless I am not ashamed, for I know whom I have believed and am persuaded that He is able to keep what I have committed to Him until that Day" (2 Tim. 1:12).

Paul said that the apostles were "fools for Christ's sake" (1 Cor. 4:10). I have been called a religious crank and fanatic. When I gave my life to Jesus Christ, some people said that it was just a phase I was going through. Well, it's been a forty-eight-year phase, and it will take me out of this life and into the next.

We are called to valor, to a life where we know where we stand and aren't ashamed to proclaim it. Jesus said, "I am the way, the truth, and the life. No one comes to the Father except through Me" (John 14:6). That's that. My life and future depend on it.

11

God, Give Us Another Chance

Blessed is the nation
whose God is the LORD,
And the people He has chosen
as His own inheritance.

Psalm 33:12

I once wrote, "I believe in my country. I cannot believe that God went to all the trouble of bringing the Pilgrims and other settlers to these shores and guiding the building of the greatest democracy the world has ever seen, only to let it be destroyed."[1]

Is it God's fault that America is following the path to Sodom and Gomorrah? No. He did not invent robots. He fashioned man and woman and gave them freedom to choose. An old hymn of the church says, "On Christ the solid rock, I stand; all other ground is sinking sand." Sometimes I think that America is on quicksand.

Years ago Roy and I rode on horseback down the streets of Philadelphia to Independence Hall. It was on Thanksgiving Day, and I shall never forget the joy on the faces of thousands of free Americans who lined the sidewalks as we passed. What a blessing it is to live in a country that is free!

As we were walking Trigger and Buttermilk through the crowds, I thought of the Declaration of Independence, a document built on the truth of God. I thought of our Founding Fathers who prayed and acted in faith. Whenever I sing, "I'm proud to be an American," I want to remember not to be so proud of our past that I fail to see that we stand in terrible need today to return to God's truth and his values that established our nation.

Which Way, America?

I was jolted recently by a survey taken by George Barna, who heads a research group that mainly assesses church trends. In his findings, based on a nationwide telephone survey of 1,004 adults, ages eighteen and older, the margin of error, Barna said, is plus or minus 3 percentage points. I'm not sharp on mathematics, but that sounds like an accurage kind of survey.

Barna warned that "in view of social trends, the United States faces one of two scenarios in the next five to ten years: moral anarchy or spiritual revival."[2]

People throughout the ages have been told by Jesus that "you are either for me or against me." Fence-sitters must choose one side or the other. If the trend we have seen in the past ten to twenty years of immorality, homosexuality, child abuse, abortion, senseless crimes, lewd language, and all of the other scum we are experiencing today continues, what will our nation be like ten years from now?

Revival or Revulsion?

Some people think that we are on the verge of a spiritual revival unlike anything we have seen since the Great Awakenings of the eighteenth and nineteenth centuries. I look at the phenomenal impact of Promise Keepers, the men's movement started in 1990 when two men, University of Colorado head football coach Bill McCartney and his friend Dr. Dave Wardell, began to pray for an outreach to men. The growth has been astounding, with thousands of men filling some of the largest stadiums in the country to hear about a commitment to Jesus Christ and to their families.

Concerts of Prayer International, Campus Crusade for Christ, the National Day of Prayer, along with small groups of concerned Christians, are growing in numbers as God is raising up people throughout this nation to pray for our country.

Many Christian leaders say they have never seen anything like it. Franklin Graham (Billy's son) said, "The churches believe that everything is coming to a head and that God is moving. Many people in the evangelical community believe that the return of Jesus Christ could be at any moment—and I'm one of those."[3]

Some believe that a spiritual revival will sweep across the land, fulfilling the "Great Commission" to spread the gospel to prepare for the second coming.

Bill Bright, founder of Campus Crusade for Christ, said, "Through the years we've seen the harvest. We've seen tens of millions of people respond to the Gospel. What's happening today has been unprecedented, I'm sure, in all of history. I doubt there has ever been a time like this."[4]

Billy Graham crusades have been growing in number across the world. His physical problems and age have not slowed down the impact of his message.

If morality is down and these positive signs are up, it would seem to me that we have an accelerating war between Satan and Christ for the heart and soul of America.

Out of the Pit

I must admit that when I listen to some of the talk shows where nothing in a person's private life is sacred, when I read of children killing parents and parents molesting children, when I see some of the sleaze the entertainment industry is serving, I want to either scream or throw up. The forces of evil have pulled us so far down into the pit that only widespread repentance and spiritual awakening can lift us out.

A prominent theologian, Erwin Lutzer, said, "There is reason to believe that only a national revival can pull us out of the ditch into which we have slid. I am convinced—as all of us must be—that every human resource is now inadequate and only the direct intervention of God can reverse our spiritual direction."[5]

I agree with Dr. Lutzer. We are always trying to run ahead of God in our desire to make events go our way.

What do we do? Vote for the people we believe best represent God's values? Of course. Roy and I have made public our stand for some politicians. However, I believe that neither a godly president nor leaders who respect the Bible and its principles will be able to reverse the direction of God's judgment.

Revival, as I understand it, means the widespread renewal of the church. The church, however, cannot be revived until individuals are revived. Jesus told Nicodemus that "the wind blows where it wishes" (John 3:8). We are not God's weatherman to discern where or how a revival may take place. But we can look to the past and see what some of the common denominators were in revivals.

What's Happened Before Can Happen Again

In the early 1700s the American churches were suffering from what Christian historians called "creeping paralysis." Into these dry and dead congregations came a powerful preacher, Jonathan Edwards. New life spread from families to churches to towns.

I was excited to find out that while Edwards was preaching, the Lord brought George Whitefield, an Englishman, who was a pioneer in the English revival, to America. Whitefield went on a whirlwind, six-week tour that resulted in the most general awakening the American colonies had experienced. One effect of Whitefield's visits was to rouse the ministers. He said, "The reason why congregations have been so dead is because dead men preach to them."[6]

What was called the "Second Awakening" began in 1857. This is how it happened.

In the middle of the nineteenth century, when our nation was divided over the issue of slavery and people had a selfish, materialistic approach to life, God raised up Jeremiah Lamphier to lead a revival of prayer. In 1857 he began a prayer meeting in the upper room of the Old Fulton Street Dutch Reformed Church in Manhattan. Beginning with only six people, the prayer meeting grew until the church was filled with praying people. By February 1858, nearly ten thousand people a week were being converted. The impact of these prayer meetings spread from city to city across the United States. Cleveland, Detroit, Chicago, Cincinnati—city after city was conquered by the power of believing prayer.[7]

What was the key to these revivals?

1. A time when our nation was in need of values and valor.
2. A few men who were inspired to reach people with the gospel of salvation by faith alone in Christ.
3. Prayer that started at home, spreading to the churches and then to cities.

Ours Is a God of Another Chance

When I was "playing like a Christian," God was patient with me. When I truly repented from my sins, he directed me to a better way of life, a better relationship with those I love, and a better long-term future.

The Bible says: "The Lord is not slack concerning His promise, as some count slackness, but is longsuffering toward us, not willing that any should perish but that all should come to repentance" (2 Peter 3:9).

Isn't that a great promise? He places value on every life. He doesn't discriminate.

When we started this book, I told Carole that I wanted to tell the world where I stand. I am not alone. Thousands throughout America are praying for repentance and revival. Will you join us in this mighty prayer?

"If My people who are called by My name will humble themselves, and pray and seek My face, and turn from their wicked ways, then I will hear from heaven, and will forgive their sin and heal their land" (2 Chron. 7:14). When God speaks about national change (as he did to the nation of Israel in the Old Testament), he speaks to his own people. We are seeing the tide begin to turn today.

The daily news may depress us, but the good news is that God may yet restore America to health.

Roy and I may be in the twilight years of our lives, but I believe this is the most glorious time to be alive!

NOTES

Chapter 1: **WHO BURIED AMERICA'S VALUES?**

1. Peter Marshall and David Manuel, *The Light and the Glory* (Grand Rapids: Revell, 1977), 17.
2. Martin Marty, "The Clamor over Columbus," *Christian History* 11, no. 3, 19.
3. Marshall and Manuel, *The Light and the Glory,* 128.
4. Thomas J. Fleming, *One Small Candle: The Pilgrims' First Year in America* (New York: W.W. Norton, 1963). Quoted in Marshall and Manuel, The Light and the Glory, 144.
5. *Christian History* 7, no. 3.
6. Sally Buzbee, "U.S. Students Score Poorly in American History," *Santa Barbara News-Press,* 2 November 1995, p. A3.

Chapter 2: **VALUE OF OUR AMERICAN HERITAGE**

1. Marshall and Manuel, *The Light and the Glory,* 285.
2. William J. Federer, *America's God and Country Encyclopedia of Quotations* (Coppell, Tex.: FAME Publishing, 1994), 641.
3. Marshall and Manuel, *The Light and the Glory,* 341.
4. Federer, *America's God and Country,* 648.
5. Marshall and Manuel, *The Light and the Glory,* 343.
6. Federer, *America's God and Country,* 380–83.

Chapter 3: **IS TRUTH DEAD?**

1. Allan Bloom, *The Closing of the American Mind* (New York: Simon & Schuster, 1987), 25–26.
2. George Barna, *Baby Busters: The Disillusioned Generation* (Chicago: Northfield Publishing, 1994), 66.
3. *Time* (5 October 1992), 34.
4. *Modern Maturity* (November–December 1995), 12.
5. *Bible Society Record* (July–August 1969).

Chapter 5: **VALUE OF TOUGH TIMES**

1. Billy Graham, *Hope for the Troubled Heart* (Waco: Word, 1991), 165.

1. Clebe McClary, *Living Proof* (Pawleys Island, S.C.: Clebe McClary, 1978), 140.
2. Tim Hansel, *You Gotta Keep Dancin'* (Elgin, Ill.: David C. Cook, 1985), 15.

Chapter 6: FAMILY VALUES IN A FRACTURED WORLD

1. *Victorville Daily Press,* 27 October 1995, p. A7.
2. Daniel Cerone, "Racy Programs Creeping into Family Hour," *Los Angeles Times,* 15 October 1995, p. A28.
3. Ibid.
4. George Barna, "The New American Family," *Moody Monthly* (September 1991), 12.
5. Gigi Graham Tchividjian, *Passing It On* (New York: McCracken Press, 1993), 56.

Chapter 7: VALUE OF FRIENDSHIPS

1. C. H. Spurgeon, *Day by Day,* comp. Al Bryant (Grand Rapids: Kregel, 1980), 89.
2. *Santa Barbara News-Press,* 5 February 1996, p. B1.
3. Dale Evans Rogers, *My Spiritual Diary* (Old Tappan, N.J.: Revell, 1955), 63.
4. Clinton T. Howell, ed., *Lines to Live By* (Nashville: Thomas Nelson, 1972), 103.

Chapter 8: VALUE OF DISCIPLINE

1. Eugene H. Peterson, *The Message* (Colorado Springs: NavPress, 1993), 474.
2. Pamela Lopez-Johnson, "Pastor takes a swat at gangs," *Santa Barbara News-Press,* 17 January 1996, p. B1.
3. Ann Landers, "Teach children now or end up with monsters," 10 February 1996.
4. Dale Evans Rogers, *Hear the Children Crying* (Old Tappan, N.J.: Revell, 1978), 54.
5. James Dobson, *Dare to Discipline* (Wheaton: Tyndale House, 1970), 52.

Chapter 9: VALUE OF PATIENCE

1. Oswald Chambers, *My Utmost for His Highest* (Dodd, Mead, 1935), 93.

Chapter 10: A CALL TO VALOR

1. Charles Colson, "Tortured for Christ—and Ignored," *Christianity Today* (March 4, 1996), 80.
2. John Woodbridge, gen. ed., *More Than Conquerors* (Chicago: Moody, 1992), 98.
3. Ibid., 181.

Chapter 11: GOD, GIVE US ANOTHER CHANCE

1. Dale Evans Rogers, *The Woman at the Well* (Old Tappan, N.J.: Revell, 1972), 182.
2. Larry B. Stammer, "Church Attendance Falls to 11-Year Low," *Los Angeles Times,* 6 March 1996, p. B12.
3. Larry B. Stammer, "God Is Up to Something, and It's Big," *Los Angeles Times,* 31 December 1995, p. A1.
4. Ibid.
5. Erwin W. Lutzer, *Will America Be Given Another Chance?* (Chicago: Moody, 1993), 7.
6. *Eerdman's Handbook of Christianity* (Berkhamsted, Herts, England: Lion Publishing, 1977), 434–41.
7. David Jeremiah with C. C. Carlson, *Invasion of Other Gods* (Dallas: Word, 1995), 189.